DO-IT-IN-A-DAY PUPPETS

for Beginners

How to Make Your Puppets, Create Your Script and Perform — All in One Day

Children delight in putting on puppet plays, and all who work with children know how valuable puppetry is as a visual aid to education, as an outlet for feelings, as a vehicle of budding artistic talent. But traditional puppet work has two serious drawbacks: it takes too long to make the puppets and too long to rehearse, so that by the time everything is ready for production the children may have already lost interest.

DO-IT-IN-A-DAY Puppets for Beginners brings a new approach, developed by the author during many years of work with children, that overcomes both these drawbacks. It shows simple methods of making puppets quickly from materials that are at hand or easily obtained, and it presents a method of spontaneous creation of scripts. By following the approach and the techniques described here, a group of children can put on a puppet production from start to finish — from the construction of the puppets through the creation of the script to the performance itself — *within the space of a single school day*. Scripts of three familiar tales are included to illustrate how the method is applied.

The creative or spontaneous technique is already widely used in full-size children's theater work but we believe that its application to puppets is presented for the first time in this book. For parents, teachers, Sunday school workers, playground leaders, camp directors and all other leaders of children's groups, it will make puppet production more useful and available than ever before.

DO-IT-IN-A-DAY
PUPPETS
FOR BEGINNERS

HOW TO MAKE YOUR PUPPETS, CREATE YOUR SCRIPT,
AND PERFORM — ALL IN ONE DAY

by

MARGARET WEEKS ADAIR

THE JOHN DAY COMPANY   NEW YORK

Fourth Impression

© 1964 by Margaret Weeks Adair
All rights reserved. This book, or parts thereof, must
not be reproduced in any form without permission.
Published by the John Day Company, Inc., 62 West
45th Street, New York 36, N.Y., and on the same day
in Canada by Longmans Canada Limited, Toronto.
Library of Congress Catalogue Card Number:
64-14127
MANUFACTURED IN THE UNITED STATES OF AMERICA

WITH THANKS

TO
K.D. AND JIM

AND TO
MY WONDERFUL YOUNG FRIENDS IN
YAMHILL, WASHINGTON, LINCOLN AND
MULTNOMAH COUNTIES, OREGON.

DO-IT-IN-A-DAY PUPPETS

IN ADVANCE

Have you realized, you who are interested enough to have opened this book, that on miniature stages in this country and in uncounted corners of the world — stages which have been set up in classrooms, camps, youth centers, hospitals and homes — certain powerful Visual Aids to Education called puppets are weaving their spell over the minds of children?

Puppets. Funny, wise, and full of rascality. Their color and motion, their third-dimensional quality, their air of having brought with them knowledge of another world, and the lure of the stories they enact, give them powerful potential for both teaching and therapy. No one denies that.

To creative children it seems that a venture into puppetry is an outlet for talent. For prosaic boys and girls, the world of the little theater affords glimpses of magic. Troubled children with puppets on their hands may find their own release. To youngsters everywhere, puppets are friends.

"If only they didn't require so much time!" teachers and other leaders are forever crying. "If only puppet construction could be made easier. Why, by the time we finish making a set of heads, our children have moved on to another story."

"It is difficult, too," they say, "to perform as often with puppets as our children would like to have us do, because of the problem of rehearsals. You know how it is. Someone catches a cold in the last hour and can't come — and there is all that rehearsing and memorizing —"

"Do-it-in-a-day puppetry," as we show in this book, has brought to us a solution of the two problems mentioned by the teachers: drag of time and loss of interest. In addition, it has revealed a greater and far more valued technique, a *creative rather than a dictatorial approach* to puppet play production.

This method wears no polish of sophistication, nor does it boast any aura of tradition; but gears itself unabashedly to the needs of the very young and springs fresh and full-blown from their wonder and laughter.

Our ways are simple. They are lighthearted ways. But they bear rich fruit; and they bring part of the "magic" of child development into full view. May we show you?

MWA

9

CONTENTS

A WORD IN ADVANCE   9

Chapter 1

     QUICK-AND-EASY PUPPET CONSTRUCTION   13
     1. Styrofoam Puppets
     2. Paper Bag Puppets
     3. Sock and Glove Puppets
     4. Puppets from Where You Find Them
     Note on Pre-prepared Puppet Heads
       and Commercial "Blanks"
     Basic Costume Pattern

Chapter 2

     CHARACTER INDICATORS   34
     Exaggeration
     Voice
     Gesture
     Sound
     Rhythm Tags
     Mannerism

Chapter 3

     STAGING MADE EASY   39
     First, A Little Theater
     Curtains
     Out-Size Properties and Others
     Makeup
     Lighting
     Music

Chapter 4

     TURNING THE TRICK WITH A SMOOTH PRODUCTION   47
     Variety in Types of Shows
     The Plane of Action
     Successive Movement
     Focus
     Surprises
     Use of Sounds Which "Tell"
     Brevity
     Use of the Right Record

Chapter 5

     ACTING UNAWARE. A CREATIVE PUPPET THEATER   54
     Step by Step as We Go. Three Plays
     P.S.   A Glance (in Passing) at Finger Puppets
          Diagram of a Miniature Theater

Chapter 1

QUICK-AND-EASY PUPPET CONSTRUCTION

For parents, teachers, Sunday school and camp leaders and others who work with children, we present four kinds of hand puppets that can make a "sudden" appearance with the greatest of ease.

Any of these may be put together and called into use in a few minutes' time. All are constructed of inexpensive, easily found materials. All are costumed from one uniform pattern which is shown at the end of section four of this chapter, and are made individualistic by means of suggested touches. In all cases, the costumes, puppet heads, and stage measurements are pre-planned to be in proportion to one another.

We show also (at the end of the book) a glimpse of the little fingerling puppets, always appealing to youngsters.

The basic materials used in making our four kinds of "quick" puppets are: paper sacks, old gloves and socks, odds and ends from the trash basket, and that popular craft material, styrofoam, now found all year around at variety stores and hobby shops, and at handcraft supply counters in department stores. Styrofoam comes in an assortment of shapes and thicknesses, costs little, and may be easily cut and tinted.

In addition to the materials listed above, puppet makers of the All-of-a-Sudden variety should have at hand these easily collected items: scissors, showcard paints, contact cement in tubes, tongue depressors or ten-inch lengths of doweling, and a bottle of water-soluble Glue-All. It is important to use only the water-soluble adhesive on styrofoam, as the quick drying cements will dissolve this material. The cements are excellent for putting together costumes and hats and so forth in jig time. Ready to use, also, should be cardboard tubes for puppet necks, pre-cut costumes in a variety of colors and trimmings, and pre-cut felt eyes, ears, noses, and mouths as illustrated.

Each of the All-of-a-Sudden puppets is presented in detail in a separate section following this one, and each of the quick simple construction steps is made clear.

1
STYROFOAM
PUPPETS

MATERIALS:

    Styrofoam balls, 3″ diameter
    Small styrofoam balls, 1″ diameter
    Sheet styrofoam, 1″ thickness or more
    Artificial hair or yarn, etc.
    Pipe cleaners
    Glitter
    Glass and wooden beads, bits of glass, little bells

An assortment of hats — either made at the moment or purchased at five-and-ten-cent store — shawls, jackets, little scarves and neckties cut from felt

Colored felt scraps from which to cut other details of the costumes

METHOD:

Apply pre-cut felt shapes for eyes, nose, mouth, ears, and the hair material to the styrofoam with Glue-All, remembering that cements dissolve the foam and are for use mainly in costume making. Tint face, or line it as desired, with showcard colors. If a hat is desired, now is the time to glue it in place.

Make a hole with a pencil in the styrofoam ball at the place where the puppet's neck will be, and ask each child to enlarge this hole in his puppet head until it fits his finger snugly. Merely wiggling a small finger and pushing slightly into the hole started by the pencil will do this.

Using a 2½-inch square of light card, roll and glue a tube which can be pushed up into the finger-hole and fit there. Glue this tube in place with about an inch left protruding to form a neck for the puppet to which his costume may be fastened.

Turn down the collar of the *front* half of one of the pre-cut costumes; apply Glue-All generously to the turned down collar and press it firmly to the front of the cardboard neck.

Turn down the collar of the *back* half of the costume; apply Glue-All generously to this turned down collar and press it firmly to the back of the cardboard neck.

Press the sides of the collar together and hold in place with a tight rubber band or with a twisted length of pipe cleaner.

For the next step, use the tube of fast-drying cement. Run a thin trickle of this cement around the side edges and tops of the shoulders on the two halves of the costume (at what would be side and shoulder seams if we were sewing) and press together. Make sure sleeves are left open for puppet's hands and that the bottom of the costume is open for the operator's hands.

At the underarm stress point or at the top of the sleeves, if it seems necessary, we sometimes use the school stapler as a reinforcement. Sometimes, if we can't wait for glue to dry, we fasten the entire costume together quickly with the stapler.

For puppets who "work" — that is who fetch and carry or lift objects in a play — *the best hands are the fingertips of the boy or girl who is operating the puppet.* Showing as they protrude from the costume sleeves, the little fingertips look very much like puppet hands, and they are able to do remarkable tasks.

A puppet who merely walks through a play without much "work" may have felt hands glued into his sleeves "for looks."

The animal puppets shown in our picture require treatment somewhat different from the above.

You will find a diagram of the cat's ears and face. She may have either felt or glass eyes, and her whiskers are painted in place or can be glued-on lengths of pipe cleaner. Her costume is, of course, put on as is described above. The small styrofoam balls which suggest her paws must be held in place with the Glue-All.

You may trace the outline of the dog and pony on the sheet styrofoam and cut them from the crisp sheet with a knife. Use the Glue-All to apply ears, eyes, nostrils, collar, harness and so forth.

Push a piece of dowel or a tongue depressor into the styrofoam so that the puppet may be held up.

SPECIAL INSTRUCTIONS:

When tracing onto the styrofoam sheet, use a piece of sharpened charcoal instead of a pencil. It is far easier to do and plainer to see.

Remember that any of the ball-head puppets may be held up on a stick instead of having the cardboard neck and being manipulated by a child's hand. There are occasions when a stick puppet is all that is needed. However, the "working" puppets are the challenge.

Make sure that your children understand they are free to assemble the pre-cut features *or* to make others which they may prefer.

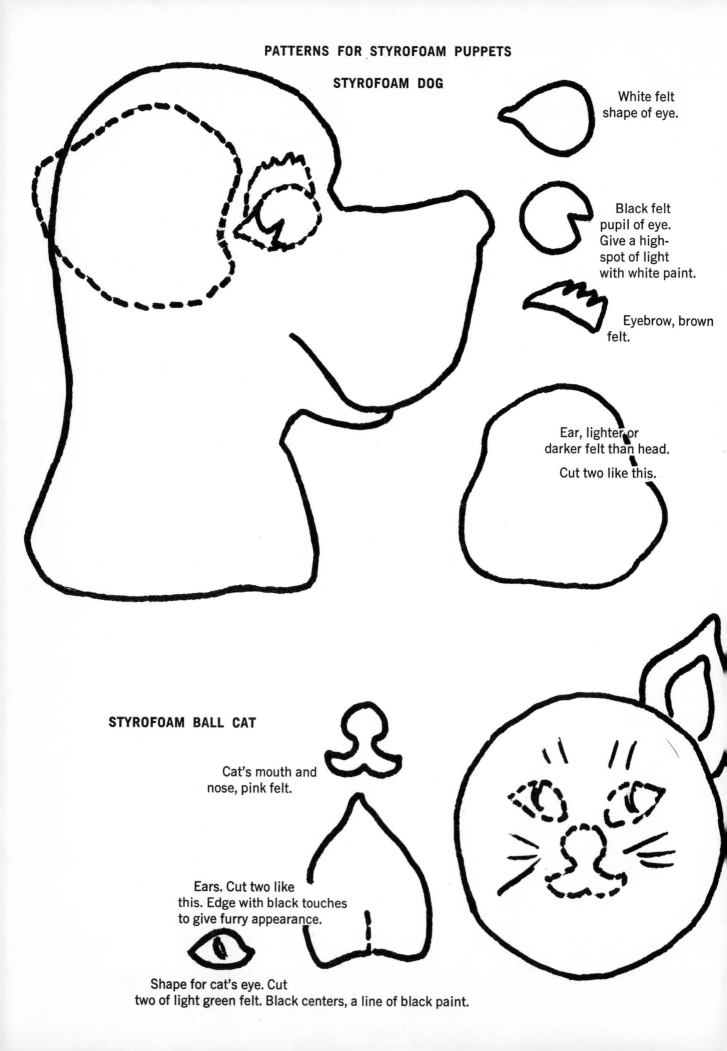

PATTERNS FOR STYROFOAM PUPPETS
STYROFOAM DOG

White felt shape of eye.

Black felt pupil of eye. Give a high-spot of light with white paint.

Eyebrow, brown felt.

Ear, lighter or darker felt than head.

Cut two like this.

STYROFOAM BALL CAT

Cat's mouth and nose, pink felt.

Ears. Cut two like this. Edge with black touches to give furry appearance.

Shape for cat's eye. Cut two of light green felt. Black centers, a line of black paint.

Eye Shape White.

Pupil of eye, black.

Nose Pink.

STYROFOAM PONY

Mouth line and spots on pony may be made with black showcard paint.

Nostril, Darker pink.

Mane, dark.

Ears, lighter or darker than head.

MATERIALS:

> Brown paper bags approximately 4″ across
> Pre-cut felt eyes, nose, mouth, ears
> Pre-cut necktie, buttons, etc.
> Rubber bands
> Pipe cleaners
> Cotton or soft paper for stuffing
> Hat and other desired costume touches
> Small styrofoam or cork balls, or buttons
> Large bandana or square of cloth for boy's costume.
> Pie-plates of paper
> Black show-card paint
> Hands of paper or felt
> Dress of paper, felt, wallpaper, etc.

METHOD:

Stuff the paper bags lightly with cotton or paper, making the faces as smooth and unwrinkled as possible, and leaving about three inches of the bag for the puppet's neck.

Run a length of doweling up into the neck, squeeze the bag-end tightly around the dowel and fasten with a tightly twisted rubber band.

Apply pre-cut facial features with Glue-All; glue on hair and hat for boy or other human characters, and pin a draped handkerchief or cloth around neck.

You may also use a smaller bag to produce a head which will fit a standard costume; the boy could be given a costume like the chick's and rabbit's, made from a second paper bag as follows:

Open the second bag and stand it on the table, bottom side up. Punch a hole in the center of the bottom of the bag, and draw the neck of the previously made puppet head (either with or without the inserted dowel) down through the punched hole. This should be a tight fit, so that the head will not be inclined to fall to the side. A few strips of adhesive tape will aid in the task of holding head and costume together.

As the picture shows, the second sack or bag, which forms a costume, may be decorated in any of a number of ways.

The two little paper-plate puppets may have painted or drawn-on faces, or their features may be cut from paper and glued in place, as are their hands.

These may be stick puppets, lifted up on dowel sticks, or may be more realistically animated by a child's hand which reaches up through the costume and grasps the puppet neck. In the case of the chick and the rabbit, both lively young animals, we much prefer hand manipulation.

RABBIT

Blue felt, to be glued on top of the white shape.

Black felt, to be glued on top of the blue shape.

White felt.

Cut four like this. Two of them pink for ear linings.

We prefer to use felt and to stiffen with glue.

Rabbit's mouth and nose. Pink felt.

Necktie of cloth or paper.

LITTLE CHICKEN

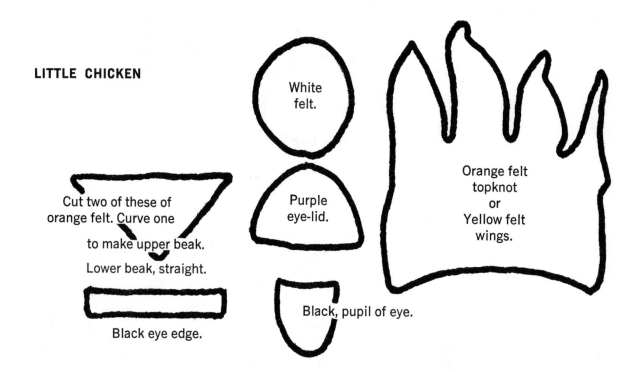

Cut two of these of
orange felt. Curve one
to make upper beak.
Lower beak, straight.

Black eye edge.

White
felt.

Purple
eye-lid.

Black, pupil of eye.

Orange felt
topknot
or
Yellow felt
wings.

PAPER BAG BOY

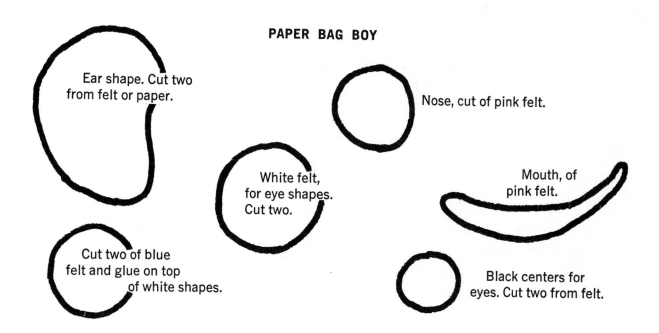

Ear shape. Cut two from felt or paper.

Nose, cut of pink felt.

White felt, for eye shapes. Cut two.

Mouth, of pink felt.

Cut two of blue felt and glue on top of white shapes.

Black centers for eyes. Cut two from felt.

An unlimited number of other characters also can be made of paper bags. By using the candy-sack size, heads will fit a standard costume like the pattern given in this book.

The bag puppet boy shown is supported by a bottle and has a stick or rod in his neck. The bottle is only for "having his picture taken," but the rod is to operate him.

MATERIALS:

Children's socks (not too full of holes). Also larger socks, stockings, and tubes of material approximately stocking length and width

Old gloves and mittens
Glitter
Buttons of glass, wood, etc.
Pipe cleaners
Artificial hair, wool, yarn, etc.
Odds and ends of hats, scarves, ties, other accessories
Pre-cut felt eyes, noses, mouths, ears, tongues, etc.

Also pre-cut felt shapes for eccentric faces such as the Wizard of Oz lion and the sea creature made of a glove and for the dozens of other animals your children will think of. It is easy to cut shapes like those in the book illustrations of the stories used, or even to cut out pictures and after reinforcing them, glue them on the sock. Use either light card or heavy cloth for reinforcement.

26

METHOD:

Slip the sock or glove over the child's hand. He is to make marks where ears, eyes, nose, mouth and hairline are to be.

Remove the sock (or glove) from the child's hand and lay it flat on the table. Slip a piece of card up into the head while you work, to keep glue from soaking through.

Using Glue-All, fasten all features in place as marked.

Remove the protective card from inside the sock and replace it with a small loose wad of soft paper, pushed up into the sock's toe; then pull the sock down over the neck of a soft-drink bottle. This gives the puppet a stand-up position when he is finished, and makes costuming easy.

In the case of the Friendly Dragon at the left of the picture, we used an open tube of material instead of a stocking because we wanted the dragon to be shiny green and to have a very wide-open mouth.

With the smaller monster made of a brown sock it was not necessary to cut the sock material, as the red felt stiffened by the glue was sufficient to make a workable mouth when a small hand inside the sock was assisting. Four fingers of this hand, of course, formed the monster's upper jaw; the thumb manipulated his lower snappers.

Following are outlines of the Dutch boy and other shapes needed to make these puppets.

PATTERNS FOR SOCK AND GLOVE PUPPETS

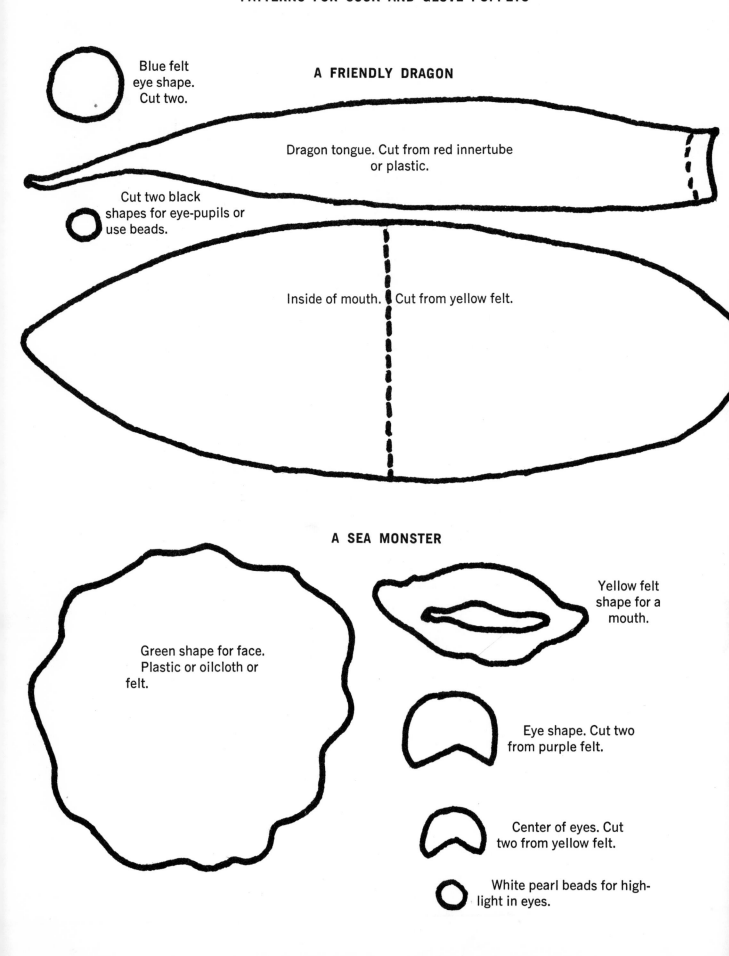

Blue felt eye shape. Cut two.

A FRIENDLY DRAGON

Dragon tongue. Cut from red innertube or plastic.

Cut two black shapes for eye-pupils or use beads.

Inside of mouth. Cut from yellow felt.

A SEA MONSTER

Green shape for face. Plastic or oilcloth or felt.

Yellow felt shape for a mouth.

Eye shape. Cut two from purple felt.

Center of eyes. Cut two from yellow felt.

White pearl beads for highlight in eyes.

WISE OLD BIRD

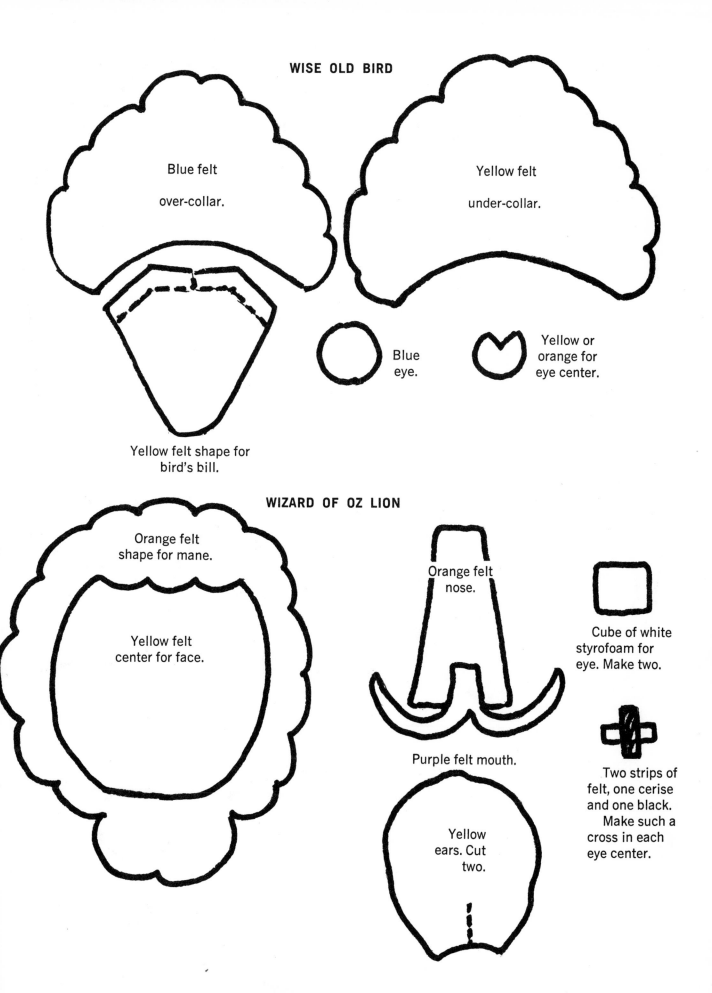

Blue felt
over-collar.

Yellow felt
under-collar.

Blue
eye.

Yellow or
orange for
eye center.

Yellow felt shape for
bird's bill.

WIZARD OF OZ LION

Orange felt
shape for mane.

Yellow felt
center for face.

Orange felt
nose.

Cube of white
styrofoam for
eye. Make two.

Purple felt mouth.

Two strips of
felt, one cerise
and one black.
Make such a
cross in each
eye center.

Yellow
ears. Cut
two.

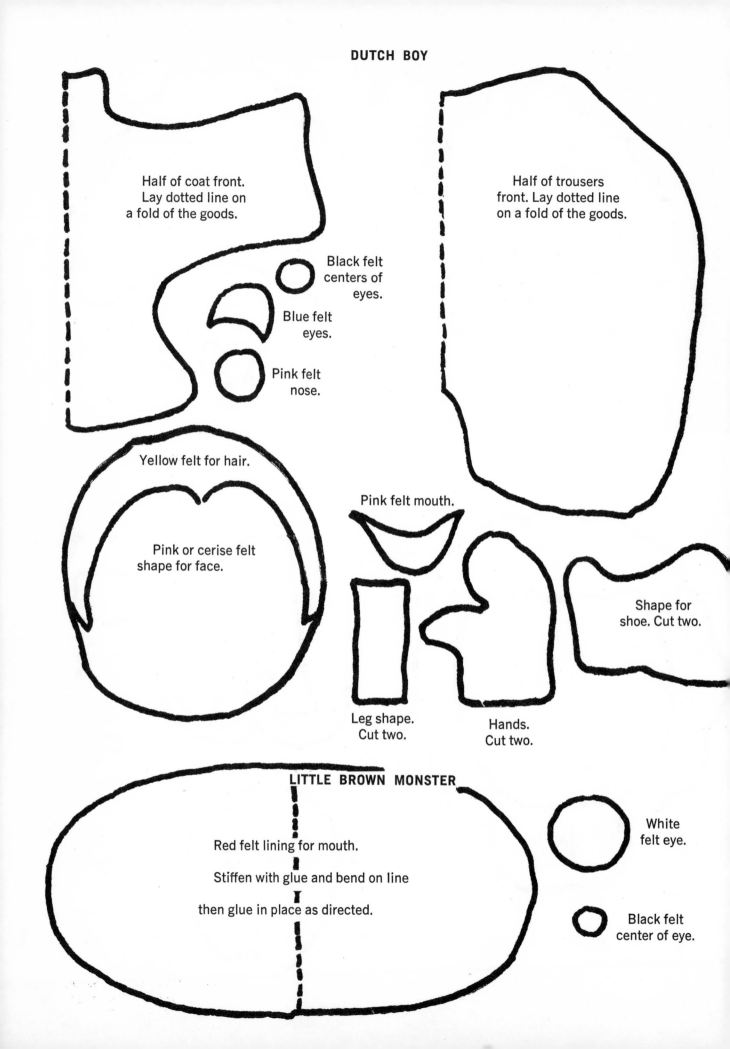

DUTCH BOY

Half of coat front. Lay dotted line on a fold of the goods.

Half of trousers front. Lay dotted line on a fold of the goods.

Black felt centers of eyes.

Blue felt eyes.

Pink felt nose.

Yellow felt for hair.

Pink or cerise felt shape for face.

Pink felt mouth.

Shape for shoe. Cut two.

Leg shape. Cut two.

Hands. Cut two.

LITTLE BROWN MONSTER

Red felt lining for mouth.

Stiffen with glue and bend on line

then glue in place as directed.

White felt eye.

Black felt center of eye.

MATERIALS:

First Woman: Wooden spoon, curly metal pot cleaner (hair), button eyes and nose, pipe cleaner mouth. Dress is a scrap of ribbon and a twist of gilt paper (or use whatever is at hand).

Sea Serpent: Green rubber hair-spray and hose, felt face, eyes of felt circles on which are glued styrofoam balls (small size) with glass bead centers.

Dog: A floor duster, with eyes made of two green Christmas tree balls on which are painted black spots, nose which is a small wooden block, and tail of a hank of raffia or shredded paper. Use a brick or piece of wood to support the mop and give shape to the animal.

Second Woman: Wooden spoon, features cut from felt and glued on, shredded yellow cellophane hair, crepe paper dress, hat of a paper cup.

Animal: Large metal funnel, black sock with foot cut off to make opening for operator's hand, small styrofoam balls dotted with black make eyes.

Third Woman: Wad of paper napkins fastened at neck with a rubber band and slipped over the neck of a pop bottle. Features are of cork scraps, arms formed by a single soda straw. Costume a paper plate and a handkerchief, hat a paper drinking cup trimmed with old toothbrush or any oddity.

Animal: Vegetable brush, wooden knob, rubber finger-stall. Eyes are colored felt discs and white pearl beads.

Animal: Stable brush, glitter, feather, pipe cleaners, eyes of felt discs and beads.

Very small people: A set of plastic measuring spoons. Painted faces (or make them of felt cut-outs) and costumes glued on.

Just for fun and to encourage ingenuity, try giving your group of children scrap materials like this now and then. Include spools, small boxes, bottle caps, tubes, wire, and whatever else is within reach. Puppets seem to pop up out of such nothings.

N.B.

We have found it useful to keep on hand at all times several pre-prepared puppet heads representing a variety of ages and types, to use as "extras" when somebody has a spur-of-the-moment idea for another character in a play. There is always a child who has time and inclination to make some of these. It is possible also to purchase inexpensive puppet-head "blanks" which are long lasting and useful to keep in reserve.

The blanks are heads molded with any desired features but without hair or coloring. They may be completed with any paint at hand.

A basic pattern for a puppet costume will be found on the next page. Unlimited variations in color, trim, etc., are possible. It is important that the curve of the top of the sleeves from point of shoulder to neck be retained, as this gives necessary leeway for an operator's hand without pulling the costume from the neck.

BASIC COSTUME PATTERN

Fold collar here.

Hand goes this far
into sleeve. May be made
double like a glove, or
used singly and glued in
place to front of sleeve.
Preferably, use no hands except the fingertips of the operator.

Cut here for jacket length.

Full size costume for use with puppet heads which

fit the hands of children pre-school and primary ages.

Cut two shapes like this.

Sew together prior to children's need of them or use

method suggested in section on styrofoam puppets.

Chapter 2

CHARACTER INDICATORS

A quick touch here and there as a result of an exchange of ideas between the children, can intensify the essential meaning of the puppet characters and turn them from mediocre to strong and sharply defined individuals. The teacher will at first have to guide these suggestions, but as the youngsters progress in their education in the theater arts and grow in power of observation as well as in the sure knowledge of "what works best," they will become independent in their judgment. These are some of the touches for indicating character:

Exaggeration to bring out some one single feature more than the others. This is an effective trick for tagging or labeling a personality, which by its repeated use becomes his trademark and results in an audience reaction of "anticipation" of his actions and responses and thus more enjoyment.

Examples of such trademarks are the jaunty cane and top hat, a pair of gloves, feet too large and too flat, an enormous nose or outsize pair of hands, spats, a cigar, a lorgnette, scarf in hand, baggy pants, trenchcoat and sunglasses, a pipe, large square teeth and eyeglasses, an ever-present umbrella, hair of a strange color or style, unusually huge or protruding ears, a flower in the buttonhole. Does not each of these props suggest an attribute of character or personality? If used persistently, does not each one say about the actor that he is jaunty or prosaic, timid or bold, dramatic or dull, conservative or imaginative? Combined with other indicatives, do these prop tags not say that this certain character is a possible hero or a possible villain?

34

A hat, too, can tell tales on the individual wearing it. Hats are easily made indicative of personality or of mood. From bowler to top hat to sunbonnet, each says something. With a backward tilt or a scoop over one eye or worn straight on, a hat becomes a tag which no audience will miss. An entire play might be staged with no special costuming except a change of hats!

Voices are character indicatives of greatest importance. Their value however is too often lost in an amateur production because of an almost universal tendency among both children and inexperienced adults to make puppet voices shrill and squeaky. Because the puppet is tiny, they think, the voice is tiny. What a wonderful opportunity they miss for strong impact upon the audience.

Puppet voices should be "human." This is the appeal of a puppet; that supposedly he feels like a human being and tries with all his tiny might to behave like one. He therefore shares the sorrows and joys of life; his handicaps of small size and awkwardness making his problems heartbreakingly difficult, his joys breathtakingly triumphant. Study an audience of children as they watch a puppet trying to lift or carry something across a stage, and you will at once see what we mean in the above statement. To the extent to which each child feels akin to the puppet he shares its problem, strains with the little character as it strives for accomplishment, and sighs with relief and smiles for it when it is successful.

A puppet is not a jumping, squeaking little creature; he is the heart of humanity. His voice should be as well placed and his speech as well enunciated and expressive of human emotion as that of any human actor, as he whispers, hisses, croons, drawls, rumbles, or thunders his words — or merely speaks in level tones.

This variety of voice, clear diction, use of dramatic pause, are as much the requirements of a first-rate puppet show as they are elements of all good theater.

A teacher in our field of work with young children keeps these elements in mind; and though she must never permit herself to "drill" upon them or to discourage the youngsters' free expression in any way or to permit her knowledge to cramp their original interpretations, her effort should move always in the direction of improvement of voice.

Gestures in all dramatization should be "big." A gesture says something by itself, without words; and quite alone it makes an emotional impact upon an audience. Or it accompanies words and makes them more forceful. In either capacity it must be noticed by the audience, and it must have time to make its meaning understood and felt.

When rightly used, the gesture grows straight out of the actor's "feelings." It holds attention which no one on stage may disrupt by untimely words or motions. Busy, fluttery gestures and the amazing jiggling, St. Vitus dance antics and perpetual motion of many amateur productions should be avoided with determination. Such jerking can gain nothing for the little character trying to make himself known, or for the play, or for puppetry in general. Strive to "underplay" rather than to "overplay" a part.

A very effective tag or personality indicative is **sound.** The constant repetition of some particular sound — a drum beat, the trill of a flute, a roll of thunder — each time some particular character is presented, soon associates meaning with that character. Examples of this kind of tagging are the gunshots preceding Western movies, Tinkerbell's bell sound in the Peter Pan story, the soft chords on strings to introduce a folk singer and so forth. Other effective sounds to use would be the shrill of a whistle, splash of water, squeak of a door, barking of a dog, drag of chains, tap of heels, clump of a wooden leg, sound of wind, tramp of many feet, sound of a car motor, a galloping horse, and the fanfare of trumpets. There are many others; but let us not overdo a good thing.

Occasionally employed, and most pleasing and effective, is the **rhythm** tag for character. Even for the most amateur performance this character indicative has proven easy to use and suitable for variation. It is worth your experimentation; but to begin with is handled with small instruments from the toy orchestra as follows:

Have at hand a different instrument for each of the characters involved. Say, for example, that in the play at hand the players are a camel, a cat, a handsome hero, and a beautiful princess. For each entrance and exit of all of these and for every movement they make, there is rhythmic accompaniment.

For the camel, we hear a heavy, clomping drum tone — "boom, boom-boom, boom, boom-boom." The cat's accompanying rhythm is the whispering "shush" of sandpaper blocks rubbed together as she walks, and perhaps a crash on cymbals or xylophone as she pounces. For a handsome hero's stalwart walking, a strong and steady beat of wooden mallet on woodblocks. And light tripping taps on woodblocks, or a staccato "rat-a-tat-tat, tap-tap, rat-a-tat-tat, tap-tap" on the small triangle, are appropriate to the self-conscious tripping steps and self-conscious posings of a princess.

This is great fun. It has many unexplored possibilities.

Mannerisms are appealing tags for establishing individuality. Give a child puppet, for instance, the habit of always saying "bread and butter" when something comes between himself and a friend, or of always getting his shoes on the wrong feet, or forever singsonging or whistling as he walks along. Make a puppet man scratch his nose or push back his hat or twirl his cane or shake his fist or bow from the waist every time he says something — cause an old puppet woman to straighten her spectacles or clutch her shawl — a young girl to pat her hair — a kitten to yawn — a little dog to turn three times around before he lies down. Have a character do any of these or a hundred other things and have him do them over and over again, and your audience will come to watch for them with amused anticipation. Often one child will share his amusement aloud, as one boy did in regard to the dog.

"Now look!" this youngster told his neighbors in the audience. "He's going to turn around three times. He has to. Or he can't sleep!"

You will remember, of course, that we do not overdo this trick of hanging tags on our characters any more than we permit them to overdo the playing of their parts. We use all the little tricks for sharpening characterizations in reasonable amounts — sparingly, effectively, tellingly.

To simplify the problem of producing the first two or three plays, when attention to voice, gesture, plane of motion, and the rest may be more than an average group of children can handle, we always begin work with Pantomime or Pantomime Shadows.

Since no child need speak, and can give full attention to the manipulation of his puppet, the actions of the puppets receive the fullest attention in this kind of production. No form of theater is more valuable as a training ground, while at the same time rich in satisfaction to the players themselves. And of all forms, this one is easiest to handle from the point of view of staging, because speech and story interpretation do not depend upon the young players but are in the hands of experienced aids. That is, they are contributed by a Reader or Storyteller, by a Singing Chorus, or by a Choral (Chanting) Group, any one of which may be seated or standing just off stage. The puppets on stage, either under the usual effects of lighting or as shadows thrown on a panel as described in Chapter Four, act out the story silently as it is unfolded. Character now must be indicated through the eyes of the beholders and through offstage sounds including the voices of the storytellers.

One point to remember, which may as well be brought out here as anywhere else because it often affects pre-planned characterizations, is that surprises are not always for the audience. The whole art of puppetry is subject to surprises from beginning to end, many of them affecting the puppeteers.

Such unexpected happenings as the broken record which is an integral part of the show to be given, the worn out light globe or wrong type of light circuit, lost and strayed properties, last-minute notifications that so-and-so is unable to come and help — and the always possible pranks of the puppets themselves when some one of them perversely takes on unplanned characteristics, waltzes off with a part he never before has played and speaks words he never before has been known to say. This happens. All of these "surprises" come to all puppeteers who work for a while with the little clowns, and to be able to take them in stride and to go on with the show to a logical conclusion is something each must learn to do.

38

Chapter 3

STAGING MADE EASY

First, A Little Theater

The most satisfactory puppet theater our Kindergarten ever had was one the children set up by pushing an empty bookcase against the front of an open doorway. The shelves facing the children gave them a place to lay their puppets and props, and the door frame itself served as a generously proportioned proscenium arch to which scenery and lights could be firmly attached. The space between the bookcase as it stood in front of the door frame and the scenery which was tacked to the rear of the frame was adequate for the play action of the puppets, except for entrances and exits at each side.

This small drawback was overcome when we applied a coat of glue to the back of the scenic panel (canvas), giving the material a backward curve as it dried, then placing standing flats on either side to mask the curve and provide "wings." (See directions at end of the book.)

This stage set in a doorway had the additional advantages of not only permitting the young players to sit or kneel on rugs on the floor, but of separating them so completely from the eyes of the audience that they could exchange places easily without being observed, thus making the illusion of a puppet world convincing.

In Primary Grades, our first choice of the theaters we set up would be the one made of a single plywood panel. This panel had an opening 24 inches high by 45 inches wide cut in it to form the proscenium or stage arch, and had a little shelf fastened behind the opening to serve as a stage floor, a place to set up necessary furniture or other props. With this theater the children manipulating the puppets are in a standing position.

The backdrop in this case was made of several layers of a transparent material (scrim, gauze, etc.), through which the child puppeteers were able to watch their own action with the puppets but through which, since they themselves were in darkness, they could not be seen by the audience.

There are two satisfactory ways of supporting such a panel. It can be done with screendoor hooks, one at each of the four corners, which slip into screw eyes in the floor and in the ceiling or whatever is overhead, such as a beam or panel. It can also be done with side braces and guy wires over which blankets, burlap or other material may be hung.

In many instances, such as in Sunday school or for an impromptu performance in a living room, or any time when not fully prepared, we have found the edge of a table or desk or the top of a room divider adequate staging for a little show. This is also one of the times when small finger-puppets may be used. Of course, the puppeteers are faced in this instance with the necessity of using a jump-up entrance and exit technique instead of the preferred walk-on, since there is no proscenium or side masking as a rule, but smooth handling can overcome part of the abruptness, and a wise choice of plays will lead to the presentation of one not easily marred by the jumping on and off. (See Chapter 4.)

Simple though they are, these desk-top, table and divider presentations, in the hands of people who will make use of their voices to the best advantage and who have been taught the value of pace, of pause, and of gesture, seem satisfying to child audiences. We think you will be amazed, as we always are, by the number of children in every group who possess natural qualities of showmanship and who need little more than an opportunity to do good work. We believe you will be awed — and not a little humbled — to observe the sensitivity and awareness of even young children to shadings and subtleties in dramatization.

For those who wish permanent puppet stages, there are a number of choices this side of hiring a professional craftsman. Some will construct frames of light aluminum pipe and pipe-fittings and will hang these about with curtains on rings. Some will use packing cases like those in which refrigerators and other large pieces of equipment come. Others may make little stages from picture frames set up on legs, or from old television or radio cabinets. A cardboard puppet theater is now and then offered commercially.

One group of teachers led young children to present plays in an unusual manner by showing the puppet performance through a door or a window of some property from the play. For instance, a Dutch dramatization was shown through the doorway of a huge cardboard windmill, the Three Bears story was seen through the casement window of a cardboard house, and Nursery Rhymes were enacted by little puppet characters who appeared as illustrations on the pages of a giant cardboard replica of a book.

Our own portable puppet stage at the moment is a three-panel screen. The center panel is hinged at about center and will fold to approximately card table size for ease in carrying and storage. The two side panels are detachable, and are constructed of light frames covered with cloth and painted. (See diagram and instructions, pages 88, 89.)

Then Curtains

Stage curtains made of window shades set to roll downward instead of upward, so that the operator is not visible to the audience, and curtains which draw to the sides by hand or which run smoothly and invisibly on traverse rods, all are feasible. And, of course, there are curtains of on-and-off lights, which lack nothing in dramatic quality.

Our own three-panel stage has curtains which draw to the sides on a traverse rod and can be opened or closed by the same operator at the same side of the stage. These curtains have weights sewed into their hems to give them a smooth swing, and the pull cords are marked to show "open" and "close" so that the operator will not hesitate in deciding which to pull.

Just behind the traverse rod we have set another rod over which scrim can be hung or stretched. This material, arranged in a desired number of thicknesses or layers, is used when giving

Shadow Plays (Chapter 4) and for underwater effects. It also lends mystery to scenes when that quality is desired.

Some Properties

Scenes and props in puppetry are held to the minimum. The modern manner of suggestion, of significant rather than full literal representation, is made to order for the tiny theater; and some puppeteers claim the technique is in fact an extension of their own pioneering. This "basic truth" and "significance," expounded by adult theater today, they declare to have been from the beginning, and with even more sophisticated artistry, their own technique.

However this may be, we do hold back on clutter. We make use of remembered experiences of the audience and we make the most of a few significant properties. Following are some of the ways of doing this:

Draw scenes on with chalk. A window or door. Some potted plants. A cupboard with food or dishes. A witch's hat and broom in the corner. The youngsters put them quickly on stage by drawing them on the canvas, paper or board of the back wall.

Does the play take place out of doors where a tree is required? Or a house or a mountain or a moon? Colored chalk will set them up in no time at all. Or they may be painted in place with water-paints in bright bold strokes, or cut from paper and pinned in their places.

In a situation where close-ups are required and perhaps are to be actually used, such as a chair to sit in or a cradle to rock, reality is necessary. These properties are set up on the shelf which serves as the stage or are supported by wooden arms extending out from the sides, and placed so that they do not interfere with the puppets' action and traffic. Each case of this kind presents a small individual problem in support, which is solved with lengths of lath, fine wire and tacks.

Other properties, those which are actually used by the small actors, are NOT IN SCALE with their size, but are given to them in man size. You will at once see why this is done.

42

Puppets, you remember, are trying to be like people. They *feel* like people! They bring no tools with them and must use ours, which they do to the best of their ability: with courage and cheerfulness. Herein lies a puppet's charm and his greatest appeal.

Does one of the small characters, for instance, love some human enough to wish to make a birthday cake for him? He will have to work hard. He must drag forward a mixing bowl which for him is as big as a bathtub, will need to fetch a great wooden spoon, must carry an eggbeater which makes him stagger. The ingredients of the cake can be imagined, but the stirring is real and is as hard work for the cheerful little puppet as if he were mixing cement with a shovel. Of course if all this work and happy planning result in a real cake for an actual birthday, the small cook's popularity rating soars high.

There are many appealing situations of this kind, in which out-size properties are part of the struggle; for example, the little artist who puts on his cap and with full-size color jars and a brush as tall as himself attempts to paint a picture to surprise someone; the tiny hero who risks his own life for a helpless baby bird or chick or to rescue a lost kitten, all of whom appear to him as the offspring of giant animals; the small fellow who must call for help to save someone, over a telephone so big and heavy that to have it slip and fall would certainly be fatal for him.

These situations and others like them are the material from which attractive puppet plays are woven for the delight of children and for their learning.

Stage Makeup

Puppet faces in school and playground plays are not "made up" with paint and powder for each performance as are the faces of real actors.

These small players, like the scenery they use, are painted once and for all in broad strokes and bold colors; and they remain the same, during the play and after it is over, as they were when the curtains opened.

As a rule a puppet face expresses one single attribute of character or one dominant mood, such as nobility, wisdom, boorishness, mischief and so forth. Occasionally one is seen which, like the Mona Lisa, expresses complexity and remote character.

However, simple or complex, remote or surface deep, a puppet takes on mystery with the play of lights on his face. Now his still features and flat eyes, his whole little being, pulse with life and warmth. Responsive in the play of light, he laughs or cries and suffers or triumphs in the story he is telling. Craftsmen for ages have carved or molded puppet faces in their flat angular planes and surfaces and painted them boldly for this purpose — that they may catch this wonderful changeable effect. However, our simple "sudden" puppets also have ability to respond to the play of light. We must not forget this important fact.

Knowledgeable Lighting

No one argues the importance of stage lighting for an evening performance, but many people must be convinced that it is important to use lighting for daytime theater. This is often a point of disagreement, often the reason a little show fails to be impressive.

Knowledgeable lighting of the puppet theater costs little and requires no specialized training. Like other aspects of All-of-a-Sudden puppetry, it is a matter of doing a few simple things right and at the right time. Lighting, you see, not only brings out the scenery; often it *is* the scenery, and the sole means of establishing a mood.

Consider the eerie blue illumination of a midnight garden, the warm pink glow of a morning sky as the sleeping world awakes, the eerie chill of green-lit caverns, the rich red and purple lighting of court scenes and of biblical tableaux — and the tense anticipation created by one small white spotlight as it searches a black-dark stage. For these and many other emotional effects and for the wonderful appearance of life which lighting lends to puppet faces, most of us are willing to part with the small amount of money required to purchase simple lighting equipment, for most of us consider lighting to be the main ingredient of showmanship.

The Lights

Our spotlight is not the professional "baby spot" which may be purchased and used with wonderful effect; it is a flashlight held in the hand. It does very well for us, too.

Instead of footlights (which glare grotesquely upon puppet faces and throw unwanted shadows behind them), we run a string of small lights up each side of the stage opening, behind the wings and out of sight of the audience. Strings of good Christmas tree lights are fine for this, with white globes substituted for the colored ones.

Overhead, immediately back of the proscenium arch, we fasten either a tubular light fixture or a fixture made of two sockets for globes. This has a reflector to send the light onto the stage, and is of course masked by the teaser or short curtain always strung across the top of a stage. Any electric store carries such fixtures, for use over bathroom mirrors or to illuminate cabinets and paintings. Window displays make use of exactly the lights we prefer.

For our flood lamps we spent a little money — approximately ten dollars. These units are equipped with alligator-jaw spring clamps which hold them anywhere, on a round or a flat surface, swung or at an angle. They are fitted with porcelain sockets and six feet of rubber cable. A grooved metal frame holds the sheets of colored gelatine or plastic as they are slid in front of the light to give desired effects.

It is possible of course to purchase color wheels which will revolve at the touch of a finger and make colored lighting a simple matter. In some cities theatrical supply houses rent these to their customers.

For the All-of-a-Sudden puppet theater without much money to spend, reflectors from heat lamps and other appliances can be used with good results, *provided they have been checked for safety*.

If you work on the staff of a school, your auditorium may already be equipped with floodlights and a color wheel.

As a last resort, when none of the above mentioned equipment is within reach, simply use colored light globes, changing them as needed. Never under any circumstances try to get an effect by covering a light with cloth or paper. This is a dangerous practice!

The Music

You may choose to use a piano accompaniment all the way through your dramatization, or there may be a reason why vocal accompaniment is preferable; but recorded music is the usual choice of puppeteers, and many fine records are available. A short list of the favorites among them is given in the next chapter.

Chapter 4

TURNING THE TRICK WITH A SMOOTH PRODUCTION

A smooth stage play is usually thought of as one in which sight, sound and motion combine to carry a story forward without operational fault, from first lights-on to final curtain. In a smooth production, the problem, the series of increasingly tense cries, the denouement or disclosure, and the end, all arrive at their appointed times at rapid heartbeat pace.

In puppet plays, oddly enough, this conception of smoothness does not quite hold true. On the puppet stage an occasional operational difficulty is endearing.

At that moment when a tiny puppet is struggling to do something which a human being could easily accomplish, the little troubled actor comes closest to his viewers' affections. Knowledgeable puppeteers have their puppets "do" as many pieces of work as the play will permit, and show the difficulties involved.

Have the children practice making the puppets use their little hands to lift and pick up, to perform all sorts of acts; and teach them to show that this work is oh-so-difficult for the puppet. The consequences sometimes are amazing.

Does a small fellow try to lift something heavy, as mentioned in Chapter Three? Is he doing a piece of work with no tools except ones that are man-size? Does he try to climb over an obstacle which to a human child would be easily surmountable? At once he arouses the sympathy of his audience and everyone would be glad to give him a lift. Everyone is on his side. Now and then a child calls out some words of advice, or will start forward to help before he recalls that he is merely watching a play.

No, a smooth production in puppetry is not necessarily one in which the actors have no trouble with properties. It is, rather, a play of action sometimes not smoothly executed because of the physical handicaps of its performers, but otherwise moving at an interesting pace and flowing strongly forward like a river of emotion, headed for a pre-destined place.

Several different kinds of staging are possible in work with children:

1. The Pantomime

This is one of the easiest forms to produce as well as one of the *most valuable aids to creative dramatization*. Detailed steps for the production of a Pantomime are given in Chapter Five. A production of this kind may be given with either a musical or a rhythmic accompaniment, with a Reader or Storyteller, or a combination of one of these with a singing chorus or with a choral speaking group.

In addition to the ease and attractiveness of Pantomime, it offers the advantage, because of the choruses, of making use of large numbers of participants. Nobody has to wait until another day to have his turn.

2. The Shadow Play

A form of Pantomime, offering the same advantages. The main difference between the two forms lies in the fact that lighting is arranged to come from behind the players in Shadow Theater. The action of the players is then shown in shadows on a tightly stretched panel across the stage opening. As stated previously, materials such as scrim, gauze and muslin are suitable for this panel. How thick the panels of cloth? How strong the lights? Exactly where placed? A few minutes of experimenting will tell you the answers for your particular situation, kind of cloth and intensity of light.

3. The Travelogue

A Narrator or several Narrators taking turns, tell of trips experienced. Costumed puppets with appropriate stage settings form illustrations for this narrative. Music can play a strong part here. Also dancing, either by puppets or by costumed children who perform in the room while the little theater is changing scenes.

4. The Variety Show

A form more suitable for older children than for little ones; but, used sparingly, a source of fun for an impromptu hour now and then. Hold down on staging and keep the numbers very short. This is, of course, a show of individually offered puppet dances, songs and skits.

5. Audience Participation Shows or Intermediary Participation

An audience is invariably delighted and often amusingly responsive when a puppet on stage addresses remarks to someone out front. Now and then one of the actors in a play will do this, as happened when the big bad wolf on his way to eat up the three little pigs once turned his crafty face and asked a little boy sitting in the audience if he thought he'd better go down the chimney after his "yum yum supper." "O.K." the little boy called back, apparently forgetting where he was and quite unconscious of the other people in the room, "but you're goin' to be doggone SORRY!"

The Kukla, Fran and Ollie performers illustrate beautifully the possibilities of the Intermediary technique. The Intermediary, a human, stands outside the little puppet world and yet is part of it. This half-way-between-worlds person understands and loves the puppets and often performs with them, singing, or playing an instrument for their performing, and is invaluable as a filler-in between acts and during scene changes.

6. "Straight" Drama

This is the natural and spontaneous retelling of a story by means of "acting it out." Straight drama will also be illustrated in Chapter Five.

The smooth and satisfying creation of plays by youngsters acting as puppeteers, as has been said, depends upon suitable puppets quickly made, upon clear characterization of those puppets as they act out their story, and upon efficient staging of the story action. This much we hope we have presented plainly and logically, in a usable manner.

We should now like to leave with you a small bag of tricks to smooth your way; for while it is true enough that many children are born with a sense of timing and drama and that they unconsciously employ tactics which other folk must be taught, it is nevertheless beneficial now and then for everyone to make an arrangement and a re-statement of knowledge.

1. Observe a plane of action when giving a puppet play. Teach the children to walk their puppets on and off stage as if the actors were traversing a floor, all of them on the same level, and with some attention to their comparative heights. It is correct in some types of comedy with puppets, as in the Punch and Judy shows and others, to let the little characters pop up from Limbo; but this is not to be condoned in straight drama. In Kindergarten, Primary and Sunday school plays, the puppet characters usually behave like the human beings *they* believe themselves to be, and consequently are not expected to shoot up as though through holes in the floor.

2. Try for successive not simultaneous movement. Knowing that action is necessary and most important in children's dramatizations, a teacher may be in danger of running wild in her effort to make sure that something is happening every minute in the plays her group presents, resulting in "action" which jangles the nerves of onlookers as the puppets jump and jerk spasmodically. All of us have seen this happen. Frankly, we cannot afford to let it happen if we have hope for a future for puppetry in the educational field. Such manipulation wins no friends and admirers.

Experienced puppeteers aim toward eliminating every bit of unnecessary action because they know that the attractiveness of the puppets depends not upon undisciplined activity but upon the significant things they do. You see? Significant. Not meaningless. What a puppet wants, longs for, needs, and at long last is able to have or do — humor, pathos, conflict, the chase, the victory — that makes a good puppet play. The number of times he meaninglessly bobs his head up and down or jumps toward the ceiling makes for nothing but boredom.

A good rule to follow, except in cases where confusion is desired — as in a fight or panic scene or when a story calls for a special bit — is to permit only one character at a time to move. One character moves, or speaks and acts appropriately; and the others focus their attention upon him.

3. Focus. Give attention. When one character on the stage speaks, gestures or performs a bit of stage business, have the other puppets turn their heads in his direction. Leaning lightly toward the speaker or character in action gives added emphasis to focus; as do other postures such as an arrested motion of the hand, a step halted midway. The character in focus is the storyteller of the moment, and what he says and what he does is advancing the tale. When he completes what he is saying or doing another character takes over and receives the same sort of treatment.

4. Surprise. Keep your audience wide awake with unexpected happenings and fresh interpretations like the following:

An animal unexpectedly speaks.

An inanimate object such as a table, bed, or a scarecrow, is inspired to rise from its permanency and walk.

Plants or trees suddenly grow either very large or very small, or reach out and catch hold of someone.

A human being gets into the puppets' act; for instance, a child made up as the giant in "Jack And The Beanstalk" may show his head and big hands.

A villainous little character jumps forward and startles the audience with a sudden "Boo!" or a friendly character waves "Hi!"

A human hand reaches down from Somewhere and helps a puppet who is caught, perhaps in a snare, and gives him a pat on the head before going out of sight.

Real bubbles rise upward from the stage, or snowflakes fall.

Bees, birds, or airplanes zoom across stage, swung on black threads or fine wires or propelled by wind-up springs, and are accompanied by motor sounds.

A statue, an animal, an old house, comes out of a long silence and nods or shakes its "head" or makes some other unexpected gesture; or even speaks.

A figure jumps on stage in a clap of thunder or flash of light or in some other startling manner.

5. Use "telling" sounds. We have already spoken in Chapter Two of the use of sounds and of rhythms to indicate character. To speak of them again here, as elements of a smooth production in puppetry, is to emphasize their importance. Sounds not only tell something about the characters of the players in a story, they often foretell the nature of the action which is about to take place by establishing a mood for it. For example: Sound of motor. Car appears.

6. Finally, be brief. Keep play lengths to approximately 12 to 25 minutes, and short acts 2 to 6 minutes. Alternate the short with the long, so that one is able to be getting ready while the other performs.

There are many wonderful and appropriate recordings to assist puppeteers, as mentioned at the end of Chapter Three. They may be used incidentally or may be taped along with the dialogue after a play is well shaped-up, so that in repeating the production the players need only coincide their puppets' actions to the tape recording. We prefer to give the youngsters free rein each time for improvisation, and seldom use a recorder except for occasions when entertainment is the prime object. Following is a list of favorite records:

Symphony No. 6 in F Major, "Pastoral" (Beethoven). Background music of birds, running streams, idyllic peace, and a storm.

Classical Marches by the Boston Pops Orchestra. Includes the stirring March from *Aida*, "Marche Militaire," the "March of the Little Lead Soldiers" and others.

"Clair de Lune" (Debussy). Sad, poignant dreaminess. Good for Pierrot and Pierrette posturing.

"Mars" music from *The Planets* (Holst). Sets an eerie or sinister mood, as for witches, etc. Actions may accompany.

"In a Persian Market" (Ketelbey). Warm, dreamlike, oriental.

"Caprice Viennois" (Fritz Kreisler). Quick-moving, vivacious, as for the dance of tiny finger puppets.

Overture from *The Magic Flute* (Mozart). Especially fine as introductory music for a puppet performance.

"Song of India" (Rimsky-Korsakoff). Descriptive of a warm and peaceful day, blue water, an East Indian boy leisurely washing his elephant. Useful as mood music.

William Tell Overture (Rossini). In parts. Offers a variety of moods. Dynamic orchestration covers nearly any need.

Barber of Seville Overture (Rossini). Vivacious introductory music.

"Circus Polka" (Stravinsky). Also other compositions by same composer.

"Skaters' Waltz" (Waldteufel). For the rhythm of ice skating, a ballet, etc.

Chapter 5

ACTING UNAWARE.
A CREATIVE PUPPET THEATER.

It was not in a schoolroom or clinic but on the public playgrounds of a big city, that understanding came one rainy day to a young woman recently appointed recreation director for the younger children when she saw all at once, through the wishful eyes of her charges, what was needed in that place and how to get it.

A few minutes' digression from All-of-a-Sudden Puppetry at this point to bring the incident to you will be worth the time spent, because it serves to focus on a technique of communication so old as now to appear new-born, and to point up precisely what we mean in this book by "creative theater." This is the way the incident took place:

On this morning in midsummer an unexpected shower had driven the children indoors to the protection of the Community House. They overflowed the rooms, and the two teachers in command faced a long day. Such a prospect ordinarily was cheerful enough. Days like this, offering opportunity for closer acquaintance with the youngsters, had often been a pleasant challenge on other playgrounds. Here, the situation was difficult.

In this community, few of the children understood English. They were separated from their teachers and from one another (for they had come from a variety of countries) by a language barrier which made communication next to impossible.

"Fine," muttered this one young woman to herself, trying to meet the baffled and lonely eyes looking at her. "Go ahead. You can show them some games and folk dances. You can watch their fine dexterity with basketry and weaving and clay. But how are you going to answer the question all of them are asking you — as to *why there is silence between us?*"

"All these people — cut off from one another!" she said again to herself, sitting down to do the best she could with the Peter Rabbit story. "How stupid we are in this world, not to have one universal language." Not quite meeting the watching eyes, she began. A few of her listeners would know what she was talking about. Perhaps they would tell some of the others.

It was while she was hopping around on the floor a few minutes later, with her fingers pointed upward from her head for rabbit ears and a wad of paper pinned to the back of her sweater for a rabbit tail, that the day's special little miracle began.

Lenska, one of the solemn-faced Polish children, started to smile. Then she put up her own pointing fingers for rabbit ears and began to laugh, chattering excitedly. Grins came on like lights around the room. Everybody put up rabbit ears, everybody began to talk.

Joey, a Hebrew boy; Tonia, an Italian girl; Maria from Lithuania; and a little boy named Hoi whose background she did not know, were leaders of groups which soon surrounded the teacher in her hopping, and hopped higher and farther than she ever could do. No one knew much of what was being said; but IT DOESN'T MAKE ANY DIFFERENCE! the teacher kept thinking, IT DOESN'T MAKE ANY DIFFERENCE AT ALL! This pantomime and this laughter — were international!

"Look!" the teacher cried then, a gleam in her eye; and she stepped to the blackboard, picked up chalk and drew. Crudely, because she was not an artist but only a person very much in earnest, she sketched the story of the illustrious rabbit, taking him from the tree roots of his birth through the adventures with Mr. McGreggor and back home again for camomile tea; and with her hands and face and body while she was drawing, she dramatized again the action of the tale. Everybody appeared to welcome the performance. Heads bobbed up and down or shook sidewise, and chuckles or frowns suitable to the mood of the rabbit character were much in evidence.

"Now!" said the teacher. She opened the storybook and showed the pictures. "And now — again!" She closed the book, leaned forward and began re-telling the story, pointing to the chalk drawings at each point of change and indicating that the children were to dramatize the action, which they did with "might and main."

It was a hilarious morning. And that was a hilarious summer; but profitable all around. That teacher learned about "free" or "creative" dramatization, and the internationality of the theater. The lonely children found kindred in a strange country and mastered enough English to know soon what the teacher meant by her everlasting questions:

"And how did this character *feel?*"

"What did he *do?*"

To be able to see clearly how this playground incident applies to our work in All-of-a-Sudden Puppetry, one may imagine for a moment how the chalk drawings on the teacher's board might look if they took on a third dimension — thickness — and began to move as animated little figurines, doing in pantomime all the things that were done in the story. They would look like puppets, would they not? Puppets, who speak in all languages and with any words supplied them, but who are also capable of communicating with all people in a universal tongue — Pantomime. Puppets, who speak to all children and for all children, needing no set speeches, no memorized lines or laborious rehearsals, but letting their words come naturally because they understand each character's *feelings* — and know what he would *do.*

THIS IS CREATIVE DRAMATIZATION, and is the approach we use in all our work; the reason (may we say it modestly?) for the success of many plays and the satisfaction of many children.

We show first in this book a streamlined version of "Three Billy Goats Gruff." Please take a look at the following short summary of the recommended steps to creative play production before you meet The Goats:

STEP BY STEP AS WE GO

1. Ask the children who have been elected to "do" today's play to bring their puppets (previously completed) and sit in a group near the storyteller.

2. Read aloud or tell the story to be dramatized. Give it an adequate reading with warmth and interest, but free of super-dramatization of your own. It should be light. Fun.

3. Ask questions; e.g. "Do you like this character? What made him do what he did? How did he feel? Can you understand his feeling that way?" Make sure that all give thought and express opinions.

4. Often during the reading ask each of the puppeteers to show with his puppet what the character in the story did; then get suggestions from the others and go back a second time for improved enactment. It is important at this point that the children feel the warmth and ease of the adult in charge and his appreciation of their efforts.

5. Watch sharply that this preparation period is kept short and to the point. When the moment arrives that the youngsters are bursting to try using the stage, permit them to do so.

6. Now, allowing plenty of time for the puppets' silent enactment, read the story through without interruption, keeping an even pace, refusing to be hurried or to be discouraged at this first rough run-through.

7. Repeat several times or until you have a smooth pantomime to accompany your reading. THE CREATIVE THEATER IS NOW IN BUSINESS. Very soon skill will grow, and with it will grow confidence and happiness.

Very soon, too, these children will be able to present speaking plays. The little green troupers will burst into speech most any time after their pattern of action on stage has been established, and when the motivation of "how did he feel" — "what did he do" — has been enlarged to "How did he feel and what did he do — and *so what did he say?*"

We use this routine of stage business in our presentations: Orchestral music drifts to a stop — offstage chime sounds — stage lights go on — house lights go off — curtain opens — play begins. At play's end the process is reversed.

If we use a Reader, Chorus, or Soundmaker's Group, these people walk quietly to a place to one side of the stage immediately before stage lights go on.

On we go now, to our three stories which have been adapted to the puppet theater.

The puppet characters for these can be constructed *in a half hour* on any morning; and *before that day is ended* any of the dramatizations can be presented adequately and charmingly.

THREE BILLY GOATS GRUFF

A DRAMATIZATION AND ADAPTATION OF THE OLD TALE. INTENDED TO BE USED IN ANY OF SEVERAL WAYS: 1. WITH ACTION PANTOMIMED BY PUPPETS ACCOMPANIED BY RHYTHMS WHILE A READER TELLS THE STORY. 2. AS A SHADOW PANTOMIME. 3. AS A "STRAIGHT" DRAMA IN WHICH THE PLAYERS WILL IMPROVISE THE WORDS.

CHARACTERS:

Little Billy Goat Gruff, Middle-Sized Billy Goat Gruff, Great Big Billy Goat Gruff, The Troll. (Directions for puppet and scenery construction given at end of this section.)

THE STORY: (*Stage directions given in parenthesis.*)

Three billy goats, once upon a time, lived in a green field beside a river. The goats' names were: Little Billy Goat Gruff, Middle-Sized Billy Goat Gruff, and Great Big Billy Goat Gruff.

(*The curtain opens, and the three goats are shown busy with their grass-eating; but as the reader repeats their names each one in turn gives a wiggle of his tail or a shake of his head to indicate that he is that one.*)

Little Billy Goat Gruff, Middle-Sized Goat Gruff, Great Big Billy Goat Gruff.

These three brother goats were happy together, except for one thing. They all wanted to leave the green field for a while, go across the bridge which arched beside them, and eat some of the red apples which grew on a tree at the other end of the bridge; and this they dared not do. In fact, they didn't even dare to think about doing it. (*The goats, who have turned their heads as these words were read and looked longingly across at the apples, now shake their heads and resolutely swing about so that their tails are toward the bridge and the tree.*) That is, they didn't dare to think about it until all of a sudden one morning, the little Billy Goat Gruff surprised them all — even himself — by having a thought on the subject.

"You know something?" asked the littlest goat that morning as he walked over and looked his brothers in the eye. "I think I'm going across that bridge — and eat some red apples."

"You CAN'T!" The other two goats said the words loudly, at the same time, and their heads lifted in surprise.

"Who says?"

"You know that," said Middle-Sized Goat, "just as well as we do. So don't talk silly."

"The troll who lives under that bridge," Big Billy Goat told him sternly, "won't let anybody go across."

"Troll doesn't own the bridge."

"Might as well."

"Troll doesn't use the bridge."

"Nobody uses it."

"Troll just wants to be bossy," said the Littlest Billy Goat Gruff. "Just wants to be selfish."

"That's true enough." (*The two older brothers exchange glances.*)

"So — I have decided." (*The Littlest Goat turns toward the bridge. Middle-Sized Goat jumps in front of him.*)

"But the troll is a fierce and dangerous rascal!"

"A fierce and dangerous one (*The Biggest Goat jumps in front of him.*) — full of bad tricks."

"Troll or no troll," said the Little Goat, (*He paws the ground and shakes his little head.*) "I've made up my mind." (*He advances, the other two goats step aside, and he trots trip-trap trip-*

trap trip-trap up onto the bridge. His footsteps are punctuated by the sound of a tapstick on a woodblock.)

Hardly had he trip-trapped to the middle of the bridge, when from down below there came a rough gruff voice:

"WHO IS THAT TRIP-TRAPPING OVER MY BRIDGE?" asked the gruff rough voice. The Littlest Goat shook his little head and he pawed the ground. (*Sound of stick on woodblock.*) Then he answered bravely:

"I'm a Billy Goat," he said, "the Littlest Billy Goat Gruff."

"Goat," roared the rough mean voice, "I'm coming up to eat you!" "To eat me," thinks the little goat aloud. "Hmm. I guess I'll have to play tricks on him."

"I'm thinking that you aren't very bright, Sir Troll," he called down then, believing that his brothers never would come on the bridge, "I'm thinking you don't know that my brothers are fatter."

"Fatter, hm?" The troll grumbled to himself and splashed down below for a moment. (*Sound of water splashing.*) "Oh all right. Go on and get out of my way. I'll get a fat one!" So Littlest Billy Goat Gruff trip-trapped on across the bridge, (*Sound of trip-trapping.*) ate all the luscious apples he wanted, (*Sound of crunching apples — crumpling newspaper comes close enough.*) and laughed to himself.

"They'll never come. A long wait to you, old Troll," he laughed. "A long, long wait."

The Middle-Sized Billy Goat Gruff over in the green field saw, of course, that his smaller brother had made his way across the bridge; and he decided that he too would try. He snorted through his nose and tossed his head and pawed the ground. (*Reader gives time for this action.*)

"Ha!" he snorted. "The Little Goat did it. And I'm bigger than he is." So trip-trap, trip-trap, trip-trap, out onto the bridge went the Middle-Sized Goat. (*The sound of his footsteps is heavier than for the small goat and is made with a wooden mallet on woodblock.*)

"Who is that?" screamed the troll from down below. "Who is that trip-trapping over my bridge?"

"I'm a Billy Goat. The Middle-Sized Billy Goat Gruff."

"Goat," snarled the troll, "I'm coming up there and eat you!" "Eat me, hmmmm," thinks the goat aloud. "Guess I'll have to play tricks on him."

"I'm thinking that you aren't very bright, Sir Troll," he called down, then, believing that his big brother never would come out onto the bridge; "I'm thinking you don't know that my brother is fatter."

"Fatter!" the troll screamed angrily. "Why is the next one always going to be fatter?"

"Can't say just why that is, sir."

"Oh all right. Go on and get out of my way. I'll get the fattest one." (*Sound of water as troll swims and dives.*)

The Middle-Sized Billy Goat Gruff went on — trip-trap, trip-trap, trip-trap, across the bridge. (*Repeat wood-sounds for the trapping.*) His little brother welcomed him gladly and they laughed together as they enjoyed the red apples. (*Repeat crunching sound.*)

"A long wait to you, Sir Troll!" they called to him. "A long, long wait."

The Great Big Billy Goat Gruff, still over there in the green field, saw, of course, that his two smaller brothers had made their way over the bridge without accident, and decided that he too would try it.

"Ha!" he snorted, tossing his head on which grew two sharp horns, and stamping his four sharp feet. (*Produce sounds appropriate to headshaking and stamping. Pounding on the floor with the fist, then with a hammer does nicely.*) "They got across all right, and they are littler than I am. What's holding me back?" Then TRIP-TRAP, TRIP-TRAP, TRIP-TRAP, out onto the bridge went the Great Big Billy Goat Gruff. TRIP-TRAP, TRIP-TRAP, TRIP-TRAP! (*Use a heavy drum beat for the footsteps now.*)

"Who is that?" screamed the ugly troll, no doubt sure that

now he had the goat he wanted, but pretending not to know. "WHO IS THAT TRIP-TRAPPING OVER MY BRIDGE?"

"I'm a Billy Goat. The Biggest One."

"I'm coming up and eat you!"

"Come along, Troll." Big Billy Goat shook his horns and pawed the ground, bang — bang — bang. (*Give appropriate sounds.*) "Come right on up and try that!"

The troll came. With splashing and dripping of water, with slipping and sliding, snarling and growling and angry little screams, he slithered up the side of the bridge (*Produce sounds.*) and to the top, then leaped to the deck where the goat stood.

The goat put down his sharp horns and shook his great head and snorted through his nose and came right at the troll.

"Halt!" screamed the troll when he saw the goat coming. It was too much for him. Besides, he knew he didn't have any right to be there, himself. "Now you halt, Goat!" Then he turned and jumped to the edge of the bridge — took a dive back into the river and began to swim away. (*Produce appropriate sounds, water, etc.*)

"Keep your old bridge!" the troll called over his shoulder as he swam. "I'll find a much better place. Didn't want the old thing, anyway!"

Then Great Big Billy Goat went on across the bridge, (*The sounds of his footsteps have a hurried and happy sound here.*) and joined his brothers at the apple tree. (*Sound of crunching apples.*)

Curtain

NOTES ON "THREE BILLY GOATS GRUFF"

Draw goat shapes from patterns given, with charcoal on a sheet of styrofoam, and cut out with a knife.

Paint the apple tree on heavy paper, cut it out, and pin it to the backdrop.

Cut the bridge from cardboard, paint it, set it in wads of clay to make it stand upright, or give it wooden supports.

For a troll, use any little odd toy which happens to be of "troll character" or construct from two circles of sheet styrofoam to form body and head, and add whiskers, eyes, grotesque arms, etc.

Sky and water are drawn on the backdrop with colored chalk.

To move the goats and the troll, the operator holds in his hand the end of a stick which protrudes from the center of the side of the animal away from the audience; or in the case of the troll, to make him climb onto the bridge, a fine wire runs from the center of his back up and over an invisible overhead support. Operator is of course hidden from his audience by an extra rear curtain as has been described previously.

PATTERNS FOR THE THREE BILLY GOATS

THE THREE LITTLE PIGS

A DRAMATIZATION ADAPTED FROM THE WELL-KNOWN FOLK STORY, AND MEANT TO BE PRESENTED FIRST IN PANTOMIME AS A READER TELLS THE STORY; THEN AT A LATER TIME GIVEN "STRAIGHT" — WITH DIALOGUE IMPROVISED BY THE CHILD PLAYERS.

CHARACTERS:

Mom Pig, Sister One Pig, Sister Two Pig, Little Pig Brother, Farmer Brown, Bad Wolf. (Directions for puppet and scenery construction given at end of this section.)

THE STORY:

Once upon a time long years ago, a family of pigs lived in a little house beside a country road; and these pigs had a strange adventure.

It all began on a bright summer morning — (*These words are the cue for curtain opening.*) — on a bright summer morning when Mom Pig came into her kitchen — and began to stir porridge for her children's breakfast. (*Reader "paces" slowly; gives time for the old pig to stir, perhaps to taste or add salt or to shake the stove draughts, etc.*)

Old Mom Pig felt quite cheerful and hummed a little tune as she worked — until she happened to look out the kitchen window. Then her eyes bulged with concern.

"My land!" said Mom Pig aloud, forgetting to stir the porridge and leaning forward to stare at her three children who were playing in the yard. "My land o' Goshen, those young ones are getting fat! Almost as fat as I am. I thought this house seemed mighty crowded last night. Oh dear." She set down the pot and snatched her handkerchief from her pocket to wipe streaming tears from her eyes, and began to shake and sob and to walk hurriedly up and down, up and down the room.

"Now Sister One and Sister Two and Brother Pig aren't little anymore," Mom Pig cried loudly, "and that means — that means — oh dear! Oh dear, oh dear, OH DEAR!" She walked and walked and cried and cried. Finally Sister One heard the noise and poked her head in at the door.

"Mom Pig," asked Sister One, "why are you crying?"

"Because you're getting big and fat, because this house is getting too little for us, because you'll have to build a house of your own, and oh my land o' Goshen, the wolf might get you!"

"Ho!" Sister One made a slicing motion with her paw. "No problem." She felt relieved that Mom Pig was only worried, not hurt or sick or something. "There isn't a thing," she laughed gayly, "for you to cry about."

"No?" Mom Pig blew her nose with a surprised blast and looked up. "Why not?"

"Farmer Brown will be coming by here today. I am going to ask him for something to make a house of, and I'm going to build it close by this one."

"Right close by, hm?" Now Mom Pig seemed to feel much better, and she began to smile. "You won't go away far off, at-all, at-all, hm?" She went back to stirring the porridge. "Good!"

Sister One, singing tra-la-la in a jolly little skipping rhythm, skipped back outside.

Curtain

The action now takes place in front of the drawn curtains. Sister One Pig enters from Stage R. as Farmer Brown enters from Stage L. The Farmer may be walking and carrying a load of straw on his shoulder, may be driving a horse and cart, or driving a toy truck. His load of straw is in bundles. Sister Pig listens as the sounds of his approach become plain to the audience, then nods and claps her paws. The Reader continues the narrative:

"He's coming right now," said Sister One Pig to anyone who happened to be listening to her. "Farmer Brown's coming down the road. I wonder what he is carrying today?" She couldn't wait to see, but ran to meet her friend as he came in sight.

"Whoa," laughed Farmer Brown when he saw how she hurried. "Whoa a minute. What are you doing out here in the road so early on a Summer's day, little fat pig?" Sister One made a low bow to him. Then she bobbed up.

"Looking for something to make a house of," she said. Then she stretched up and sniffed the load of straw. "Ummm. Nice clean straw, I see."

"Wouldn't make much of a house, funny little pig."

"I think it would. Could you spare a little?"

"Of course. Here. (*He tosses a generous load to her.*) Take all you want." Then he went on his way. Sister One Pig picked up the straw. It covered her face, but she managed to call after the kind old man, "Thank you, Farmer Brown!"

"You're welcome as rain!" The words came back to her as she lost sight of him.

"Now — for my house." Sister One Pig walked a few steps in the direction of her old home. But her load was prickly and the day was warm, and she was really a lazy little pig. She soon stopped. "This is as good as any place," she said, dropping the straw in a heap, arranging it with a few shoves and careless pats. "And that's good enough. I'll take a little nap." She crawled into the straw out of sight and went sound to sleep. (*To give the illusion of house being built, simply lift very slowly as the pig works with the straw the little cardboard house-of-straw shown. Have a mark on the rod or stick which holds up the cardboard house, so that it will not be lifted above stage level and appear to float. The puppet who is supposedly hiding inside the straw house, actually ducks down behind it and is below stage level.)*

Hardly had the little pig closed her eyes, when tip-toe, tip-toe, looking fiercely this way and that way, came the wolf. He gave a loud growl and knocked at the straw house door, and Sister One Pig woke up. The wolf growled again.

"Little pig, little pig," he called, sounding fierce and very hungry. "Let me come in!"

"No!" squealed the Sister One, knowing he wanted to eat her for dinner. "No, by the hair of my chinny-chin-chin. This is my little house and you can't come in."

"Then I'll huff!" roared the wolf. "I'll huff and I'll puff, and I'll blow your house down!" And that is what he did.

He huffed and he puffed; then he took a deep breath and huffed again, and away went the straw house, so that Sister One had to run for her life. The wolf leaped to grab her.

This way and that way she scurried! That way and this way! Twice the wolf's paw reached out and touched her. His hot breath burned her. Once he actually had hold of her, but he stumbled over something and she got away. She ran into the forest and hid among the trees; while the wolf jumped up and down, arms crossed over his empty tummy, and roared after her.

"I'll get you yet!" he said. "I'll get all of you pigs!" Then he slunk into the forest and went back to his cave.

ACT TWO. *Scene the same as for Act One. Mom Pig is looking out the kitchen window and watching her two children in the yard as the curtains open. When she turns toward the audience she snatches out her handkerchief, begins to shake and cry as before, walks agitatedly up and down the room. The narrative continues:*

Mom Pig knew of course that Sister One Pig had managed to get away from the wolf, but she didn't know where she was hiding.

She didn't know either, what to do about her other two children. They kept getting fatter and fatter, and the house was a tight fit. Sister Two, out in the yard, heard Mom's crying and poked her head in at the door.

"Mom Pig," asked Sister Two, "why are you upset again?"

"Because I don't know where Sister One is hiding; because you are getting big and fat and this house is too little for all of us and you will have to build a house of your own, and oh my land o' Goshen — the wolf might get you!"

"No problem!" said Sister Two, making a slicing motion with her paw. "I have already asked Farmer Brown to bring me some wood. I'll make a house of wood, close by. The wolf would have a hard time of it to blow down a wooden house."

"A wooden house, hm? Right close by, and not far off at-all, at-all! Good!" Mom Pig felt so much better that she picked up the broom and began to sweep her house, and Sister Two skipped out to the road. (*The curtains close. Action now takes place in front of the closed curtain.*)

"Farmer Brown should be here soon," she said, tipping her head to listen, shading her eyes with a paw to get a sight of him. Then she began to nod her head. He was coming. (*Audience hears him.*)

"Good morning!" she called, running and making a very low bow to her friend when he came in sight; then reaching up to touch his load. "Some nice smooth wood, I see. Can you spare a little?"

"Take all you want, you funny little fat pig," Farmer Brown chuckled. And he tossed off a nice bit of lumber for her and drove on his way. She picked up the load and walked a way with it; but she, too, was a careless, lazy little pig, and the day was very warm. Soon she put down the load, took out her hammer and nails and began to put her house together right there beside the road.

"This place is good enough," she said to herself. She nailed the boards any old way, nothing straight, nothing measured. "It's good enough," she said. "Who cares if it isn't perfect? I can sleep just as well in it." Soon the house of wood was finished, and Sister

Two Pig went into the house to take a nap. (*Use the same method here as with the straw house. Lift the replica of the house of wood slowly into position while the pig appears to be building, then have the puppet hidden as before.*)

Hardly had this second little pig closed her eyes when tip-toe, tip-toe, looking fiercely this way and that way, came the wolf. He gave a loud growl and knocked on the wooden house door, and Sister Two Pig woke up. The wolf growled again.

"Little pig, little pig," he called, sounding fierce and very hungry. "Let me come in!"

"No!" squealed the Sister Two Pig, knowing he wanted to eat her for dinner. "No, by the hair of my chinny-chin-chin. This is my little house and you can't come in."

"Then I'll huff!" roared the wolf. "I'll huff and I'll puff, and I'll blow your house down!" And that is what he did.

He huffed and he puffed; then he took a deep breath and huffed again, and away went the house made of wood, so that Sister Two had to run for life. The hungry wolf leaped after her.

This way and that way she scurried! This way and that way — and just around a corner the wolf caught her by the dress — and his breath burned her and his teeth snapped at her — and both of them thought surely he had her for dinner! But she twisted and she turned, she stamped on the old wolf's toes with her sharp little feet — and she bumped him in the nose with her hard little head — and twisted some more, and her dress tore, leaving a piece in the wolf's grasp — but she got away from him! Then she ran into the woods and hid among the trees; while the wolf jumped up and down, arms crossed over his empty tummy, and roared after her.

"I'll get you yet!" he roared. "I'll get all of you pigs!" Then he slunk into the forest and went back to his cave.

ACT THREE. *The curtain opens on a scene out of doors. A green hill, forest in the far distance, Mom Pig's little house in the middle distance. The lighting is that of early morning. Reader continues the narrative:*

For a few days after Sister Two Pig disappeared, old Mom and Little Brother Pig stayed inside their house with the doors all locked tight and the shades pulled down, afraid to budge. Even afraid to go out into their garden and pick some fresh vegetables to eat. Then they began to grow tired of staying inside like that. And they grew tired of being afraid all the time. And they grew very hungry. Little Brother Pig, especially, knew that he had had just about all he was going to stand of this business of hiding. One morning, while Mom Pig was still asleep in her bed, he opened the front door and walked out.

Enter, Little Brother Pig from Stage Right. He shades his eyes with one paw and looks down the road as though awaiting someone, and now and then puts a paw behind his ear to listen.

"This is Farmer Brown's day to come by," said Little Brother Pig to himself. "He will help me. I know he will. (*Sounds of the farmer's approach are heard.*) There he comes, now!" Little Brother Pig ran forward to meet his friend, tipped his little hat and made a bow. "Hi, Farmer Brown!"

"Looks like trouble around here," said Farmer Brown, noticing the wreck of the wooden house and the window shades pulled down in Mom Pig's house.

"That wolf has got us all scared to pieces!" Little Brother Pig told him. "He's out to catch us all for dinner. And we sort of object to the idea."

"Shouldn't wonder," the farmer nodded. "Shouldn't be a bit surprised if you objected to it." He put a load of bricks down on the road. "These bricks help you any?"

"They'll make a good strong house. I'll build it carefully, brick by brick, so and so."

"Knew you would. Wolf won't blow down any house that's built right."

"I'll make it big enough for all of us."

"Yep. That's the thing to do."

"But — we'll all be afraid to come outside of it! You just can't go on being afraid of something forever."

"Nope. Can't do that."

"I'm going to catch that old wolf! I'm going to out-think him, and trap him!"

"Hurrah! Now you're talking! You trap him, Brother Pig — I'll bring my gun and shoot him bang." Little Pig began to laugh. He reached up to whisper in Farmer Brown's ear. Farmer Brown's head nodded up and down hard, and he laughed too.

"Good idea, hm?"

"Mighty good! Go ahead with it. I'll be seeing you!" Farmer Brown went on his way, and Brother Pig began to carry his load of bricks to a place he had chosen as the best spot for his house. There was fresh water here, a tree of red apples in the yard and room for a large patch of vegetables. He carefully began his work. He planned and he measured the way the house should be, and brought plaster to hold the bricks together. He made strong doors and stout windows with shutters and locks on them.

"Brick by brick it grows," he said. "Lay them straight, Brother; so and so. So — and — so." This house was going to be made right. The last thing he finished was a fine big fireplace with a big chimney.

Of course the wolf was watching; but Farmer Brown was usually around too, and the wolf had to wait his chance.

Finally that chance came. He knocked on the door.

"Little pig, little pig," he growled, sounding very fierce and very very hungry. "You let me come in there!"

"No," answered Little Brother Pig. "No, by the hair of my chinny-chin-chin."

"Then I'll huff! I'll huff and I'll puff and I'll blow your house down!"

"Go ahead! Try it!"

The wolf huffed. He huffed and he puffed.

(In the midst of this huffing, drums roll, the lights flash and dim, and the curtains close, open quickly to reveal interior of the brick house. Show only necessary parts: fireplace and chimney, big kettle and Brother Pig ready with the lid, and up above the stage but in sight of the audience, the top of the chimney where the wolf comes down.)

He puffed and puffed. But he couldn't blow *that* house down. And how furious he was! How mean and how angry!

"Who needs a door!" roared the bad old wolf. "This silly pig has built a fine way in for me! I'll go down his chimney!" And scramble, scramble, digging his sharp claws deep, the wolf went up the apple tree, leaped over the roof of the brick house, and rushed toward the chimney opening. Farmer Brown, hiding just down the road a way, saw it all happen.

Little Pig inside his house heard the wolf coming, and he was ready for action. This was the way he had planned things. He took

off the lid of the big kettle he had set directly below the chimney, and waited.

Old wolf grabbed hold of the edges of the brick chimney, swung his black legs over — and dropped inside.

Dropped right into the big kettle waiting for him! And Brother Pig slammed on the lid! And Farmer Brown ran in and shot the wolf! (*Have wolf push out of kettle and rush to attack Farmer.*)

All the other pigs, Mom and Sister One and Sister Two, came running to the brick house when they heard the shot; and they all set up three cheers for Farmer Brown as he carried the bad wolf away. Then, safe once more and happy to be together again, they danced and sang in the good brick house. "Who's afraid?" they all laughed —

"Whose afraid of the big bad wolf — tra-la-la-la-la?"

Curtain

Stage lights off, house lights on. Reader bows, picks up her book, slowly walks behind the puppet stage. Music plays as audience leaves.

NOTES ON "THE THREE LITTLE PIGS"

Sisters One and Two and Brother Pig are made in the usual manner from styrofoam balls with cardboard tube necks and pre-cut felt shapes of eyes. Their noses are sawed-off corks painted white, their ears are heavy white paper or white felt, cut like the pattern shown at end of this section.

Mother Pig's head is a circle cut from sheet styrofoam, and the effect of chin, fat cheeks, etc., is accomplished by gluing on (with Glu-All, not the quick-drying cements which dissolve styrofoam) halves of small styrofoam balls. Her eyes are felt shapes with bead centers, her nose a sawed-off cork of larger size than those of her children, and her ears are cut from paper, felt or light leather scraps, according to the pattern shown.

The farmer, also a styrofoam head with pre-cut felt features, may or may not be given a hat, mustache and pipe.

Mr. Wolf's head is cut from heavy styrofoam sheeting. Use pattern given. Draw on the styrofoam with charcoal and cut out with a knife. Paint the head black or gray, paint the inside of the mouth red. Eyes are red felt shapes like the pattern, with small styrofoam ball halves for eyeballs centered by black felt disks. Ears are of felt, light leather or heavy paper cut according to pattern shown and fastened in place with common pins then glued. Gray or black artificial hair adds much to the character's wicked appearance. Also teeth (sticks).

The pigs wear standard costumes. The wolf is a sock (in this case a stocking) puppet. Cut off the toe of the black stocking and slip it up over the wolf puppet's thick neck in a firm tight fit, reinforced if necessary by wrapping with strips of cotton cloth and gluing.

The child operator's hand goes up through the stocking and maintains a firm grip on the wolf's neck until his tumble down the chimney, when it is not too difficult to slip the hand free.

We have added front legs or arms, made of wrapped wire, and a cape of tan felt.

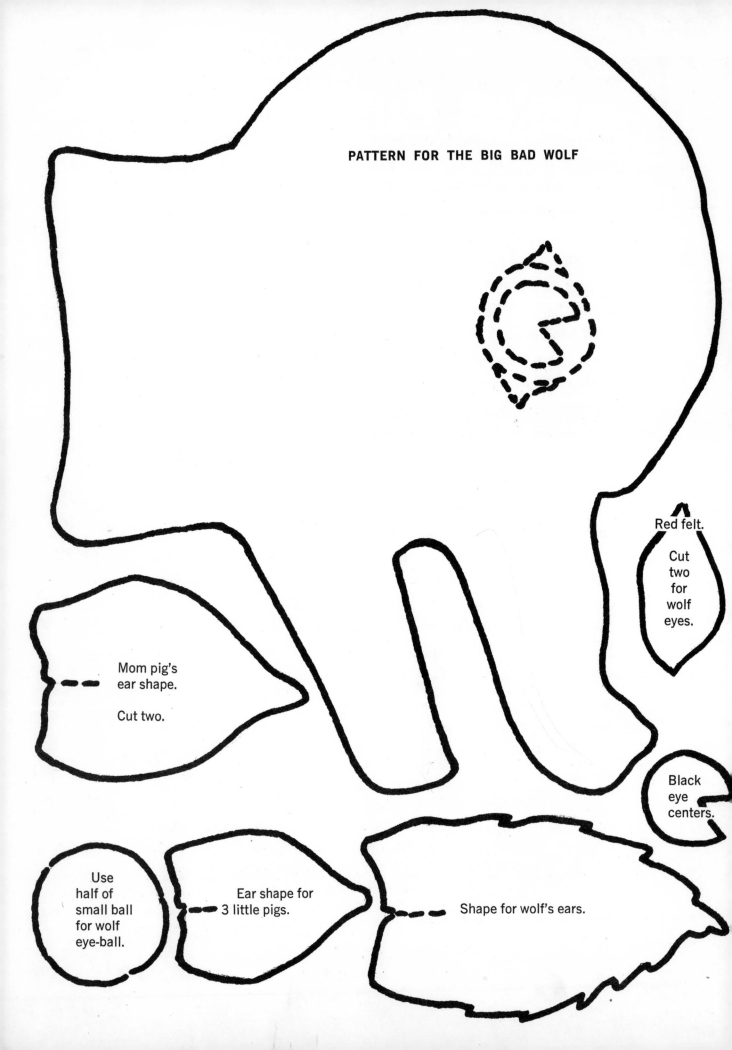

PATTERN FOR THE BIG BAD WOLF

Red felt.

Cut two for wolf eyes.

Mom pig's ear shape.

Cut two.

Black eye centers.

Use half of small ball for wolf eye-ball.

Ear shape for 3 little pigs.

Shape for wolf's ears.

KING MIDAS AND THE GOLDEN TOUCH

Adapted from a Greek
myth for dramatization
in the puppet theater.

CHARACTERS:

King Midas, Queen Penelope, Princess Marigold, The Wishing Sprite. T.V. Announcer.

Stage directions for dramatizing this story are all given in parenthesis as the story develops. Before the stage curtain opens the T.V. Announcer, a little boy who is old enough to handle the telling, or an adult "reader," walks out from behind the puppet theater and speaks into the microphone. This may be either an authentic piece of equipment or one constructed by the children.

ANNOUNCER:

Ladies and gentlemen, you are about to see the first television showing of that well-known old story of King Midas and the Golden Touch.

79

The story says that in a beautiful castle high on a hill there once lived a king named Midas; and that there lived with him his beautiful queen, Penelope, whom he called Pretty Penny, and his little girl, Princess Marigold.

This king was a good man. He loved his family and his fine country and enjoyed doing good deeds for people. But he did have one big fault — one big troublesome fault which was almost more than people could stand. Our story shows you what happened. Here comes King Midas now.

The curtain opens and the king enters Stage Left, carrying a large bulging bag with a dollar sign plainly marked on it, crosses as though to seat himself in a chair placed at Stage Right, passing through a patch of flowers as he does so. Before reaching the chair he accidentally steps on one of the flowers and stops to apologize. King pantomimes the action. Announcer continues, carrying the dialogue:

"Oh, I'm sorry I stepped on you," the king said. "This bag of gold is so big it covers up my face. I didn't see you." He set the money bag down on the chair and returned to help the flower back to a standing position. "There. That all right now?"

"Everything's all right," smiled the unhurt posy. "Don't give it another thought."

"Funny thing," puzzled old Midas, scratching his ear thoughtfully, "we've got millions of flowers around here, all yellow ones of course, gold colored like you — but I can't remember that I ever heard one of them talk before today."

"I am not an ordinary yellow flower. I was sent here today to bring you a reward."

"Why on earth should you do that?"

"Because you have done so many good deeds for the people of your country. You are to be given a wish."

"A wish! I must be dreaming. You mean you are about to let me wish for something? And my wish will come true?" The flower sprite laughed and nodded her head.

"That's right," she said. "That's exactly right, Sire. What is your wish?" The king shook his head, pounded the sides of his head with frantic hands, and walked back and forth, back and forth there in his garden.

"Why — I don't know! I just don't know what my wish is!"

"I hear you are very fond of gold. That you like everything about you to be gold color or to be named for gold."

"Yes. Of course I couldn't do too much with my wife's name because she already had been named before I met her. I do call her Penny."

"Yes," laughed the flower sprite, "I know. And your little girl — you named her Marigold. How you do love her name and her beautiful golden hair."

"Sometimes I wish everything I touched would turn to gold!"

"Oh no! No, King Midas!"

"No what?" The good king did not understand the sprite's concern. "What did I say wrong?"

"You made your wish!" cried the sprite. "You wished for the Golden Touch!"

"My word." The king began to smile, then to rub his hands together in pleasure. "I did do that, didn't I? The Golden Touch. Well what is so wrong about that?" He turned to the little sprite to ask this question, but saw that she was not there any longer. She had vanished. (*It is very easy for a child hand to remove the sprite and snatch her below stage level, or if this is not easily handled, remove the sprite by jerking her out of sight by means of heavy thread.*)

(*The king is excited. He is happy and somewhat confused; and runs here and there across the stage, touching things.*)

"She must have been telling the truth!" the king exclaimed. "At least she believed it was true. Let's see if the wish will truly work. If I touch this bush — and this chair where my bag of gold is sitting — and this rock beside the chair — and this little statue in the fountain —" (*These mentioned properties all are grouped close by. When the king stands back to watch, after he touches them, they appear to be slowly changing in color and becoming golden. This is done by the focus of a golden spotlight from offstage.)*

(The king is filled with awe. He looks at the transformation, looks at his hands, shakes his head, walks over to the chair and sets the bag of gold on the ground, then tensely seats himself in the chair.)

"It is true!" he whispered, staring about him, overcome with the vision of all the gold he could now have. "It is true. I can do it. I can have all the gold I want. Whatever I touch! Think of it! *(His wife, the queen, enters from Stage Left, carrying a plate of fruit for him. He stands to greet her.)* Think of it, Pretty Penny!"

"Think of it? Think of what, my dear?" his wife replied. "Oh let's not think of anything. It is far too beautiful a day for thinking. Here, I have brought you some of your favorite fruit."

"Thank you, my queen. That looks delicious." King Midas reached — picked up one of the fruits, then jumped back, startled and alarmed, letting the fruit fall to the ground. *(Sound of a stone hitting the floor, offstage.)* "No! Oh my stars — NO!"

"King! You look so pale! *(The queen helps him to the chair.)* There. You had better rest a moment." *(The king sits slowly, stares at her, seems overcome with his vision of the future.)*

"Whatever I touch! Everything I touch will turn to gold — even my *food*!" The queen stared around at the changes the Golden Touch had made in the garden, stared at the king's hands, then stepped back, out of his reach.

(He slumps in his chair. The queen has her back turned and is taking a closer look at the fountain statue, when Princess Marigold enters. Neither the king nor the queen know she is there. Marigold skips over to her father, lays her hand on his shoulder and leans lovingly against him.)

"Father, will you stop being an important king for a while, and come play with your little girl?"

"Marigold! *(The king leaps to his feet, the queen whirls around to stare in alarm, and Marigold retreats a few surprised steps, to a position close to center stage.*) Don't touch me, don't let my hands touch you, Marigold! Go away — go away, my Marigold!"

"Oh this is a good game!" The little girl believed that the king was pretending something just for fun. She snatched up one of his hands and placed it on her head. "What shall I be?" (*The light moves to her. She becomes still — motionless.*)

"You — will be a statue," the king whispered, overcome by his sorrow, staring at his daughter's form. "You will not be my little girl — any more."

"Marigold!" cried the queen. "Oh — Marigold, come back to us." (*The king and queen crumple to the ground, and the curtain closes.*)

ACT TWO. *The king sits in his chair, head bowed, too sad to speak. The queen stands at stage left, looking into space. Marigold's golden statue is as before, quiet and motionless. A yellow flower has grown since Act One, close to the king's chair. The bag of gold pieces lies forgotten.*

ANNOUNCER:

The king you see today, ladies and gentlemen, is not the happy man you met in Act One— not the man who enjoyed life, did good deeds for other people, and had the strange hobby of collecting gold pieces. The king is sad now. All he does is sit here in the castle garden. When anyone mentions the word "gold" to him, he rouses himself enough to answer:

"What good is gold? You can count it, you can feel it in your hands, you can save it — or spend it. But what can it buy? Can it buy happiness? Can it buy my little girl back again, for me?"

"The queen and I," he said one day, "would give all the gold in the world, if we had it, to get our Marigold back again. Oh how I wish I had never wished — for the Golden Touch!" Close beside his chair, that yellow flower which had been standing there moved and turned its little face to him. (*The flower is easily manipulated by running a wire over the edge of the stage floor or down through a small hole bored in the floor.)*

"King Midas," the flower told him, "I have been waiting — and waiting for you to say those words!" The king turned his own head and looked at her. He could not speak.

"Do you remember, Sire, when you first spoke of the Golden Touch, you used the words 'sometimes I wish'? You didn't actually want the Golden Touch, did you? Not really?"

"No, little sprite," said the king, shaking his head. "I didn't want it — really. And I'll certainly not ever want it again, even for a moment."

"Then it is gone! You are granted your second wish — that it be gone!" The king jumped to his feet — turned to look at the little golden statue which was his daughter. The queen ran too to look at her.

Slowly the quiet little statue began to move — then to smile. And in a moment, Princess Marigold was safe in her parents' arms. The three of them stood there in the castle garden, laughing and hugging one another. (*Curtain slowly closes.*)

You could hear them playing games together all the long sunshiny afternoon. Games like tag and hide-and-go-seek and hop-scotch. Games like London Bridge, and Looby Loo, and Skip-To-My-Lou My Darling.

(*The Narrator closes his book, puts it under his arm, gives a small salute to the audience, and walks off.*)

NOTES ON "KING MIDAS"

The castle is painted on heavy paper, cut out and pinned to the backdrop. Flowers also are cut from paper and pinned or tacked in place.

The king's chair may be a candy-box or a doll chair.

King, Queen and Princess are styrofoam heads with felt costumes. Ermine for king is white cotton batting with ink spots; the queen's long stole, a thin scrap of felt sprayed with light gold. Crowns are old costume jewelry or could be cut from gold paper, etc. King's shoes are carved from wood and painted. Could just as well be doll shoes from a store or be made of two felt shapes put together with glue, stuffed with cotton.

Sprite is a yellow felt flower-shape, like pattern, small wooden ball makes face, wire wrapped with crepe paper is costume. Numerous other ways of making a magic character are of course possible.

We used gold spray rather generously in the scene.

PATTERN FOR THE MAGIC FLOWER

These finger puppets are simply tubes of colored felt. They are made of felt squares 2½ inches on each edge, rolled to fit the finger snugly, and glued. Animal ears may be added as are other features, but preferably are cut as part of the original square.

Beads, pipe cleaners, decorator braids, sequins, etc., assist in accomplishing these and many other effects.

We present these only "in passing" for the reason that they are too small to be considered a true part of puppetry.

They are fun, nevertheless, in small intimate groups when viewers are close and staging is limited; and all storytellers know how much children love to have their story characters pop up unexpectedly, as only fingerlings can do.

A MINIATURE THEATER

We use this practical three-panel theater for All-of-a-Sudden Puppetry;
but many other methods of staging puppet shows are satisfactory.

A stage opening 24 by 45 inches is large enough to make plays visible in a large room, and also is in pleasing proportion to the size of our All-of-a-Sudden puppets.

Height of panels depends upon whether the puppeteers are expected to stand, kneel or sit while presenting their plays. We prefer a standing position as a rule, with a backdrop thin enough so that the youngsters can see their own puppets at work; but we often work with heads below stage level and arms stretched upward, if the action is not too long and fatiguing.

This front panel is of plywood, brightly painted. Side panels are cloth-covered frames. Panels are joined with pin hinges, easily separated or put together.

Stage curtains are opened and closed by a sash cord rigged with three pulleys.

The few "stage words" we have used are explained here, and illustrated by numbered parts in the sketch opposite:

1 Backdrop. 2 Wings or sides. 3 Teaser, a short curtain across the top of the stage. 4 Flats, or cloth-covered frames used as screens or to supplement scenery, etc. 5 Props, or properties — that is, furnishings used in a play.

Children are interested, too, to learn that the terms Stage Right and Stage Left refer to the actors' right and left.

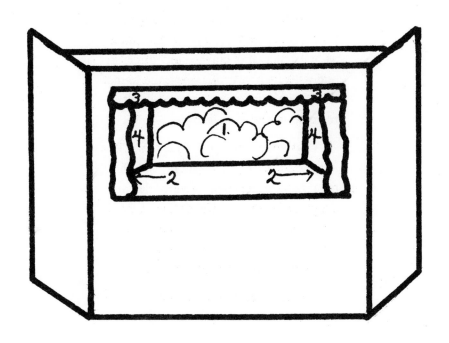

About the Author

Margaret Weeks Adair began to work with puppets early in her career as a teacher and playground director, and with each year of experience found them more and more valuable both as recreation and as therapy.

A graduate of State Teachers College, San Jose, California, she has taught and supervised playgrounds and handicrafts at the Riverdale School, Portland, Oregon, and for the Portland Playground Association. She is a member of the Puppeteers of America.

She and her husband, who live in Portland, have two grown sons.